A DIFFERENT MOTHER

2nd Edition

rena trefman cobrinik

A Different Mother

by Rena Trefman Cobrinik

* * *

Chapter III was previously published in the *Jewish Women's Literary Annual* (ISSN 1523-7672), Volume 7 (2006).

Chapter IX was previously published in the *Jewish Women's Literary Annual* (ISSN 1523-7672), Volume 4 (2000-2001).

They appear here with thanks to the editor, Dr. Henny Wenkart.

Book design by Ann Eisenstodt
Edited and formatted by Gail Kaliss

cover photo: Anna Kreminetsky Trefman, 1918

* * *

Library of Congress Control Number: 2017912553

CreateSpace Independent Publishing Platform
North Charleston, SC

To my mother

who was in love with life

A DIFFERENT MOTHER

Contents

	Preface, by John A. Russo, M.D.	vii
	Prologue	ix
I	Elmhurst, Queens	1
II	Old Times	9
III	Visit to Becky Lieb	21
IV	Contradictions	33
V	Leaving Elmhurst	45
VI	The Picture over the Couch	61
VII	Applying for Sunnyside Lodge	73
VIII	I Learn about Dementia	81
IX	My Mother Had a Lover... A Hideaway	95
X	Life at Sunnyside Lodge / Morningside	105

XI	The Nicest One	119
XII	The Third Floor: Kindness in Abundance	129
XIII	The Rose Garden: Is He My Father?	143
XIV	Two Visits	155
XV	A New Mother	167
XVI	Jacoby City Hospital	175
XVII	Back to Morningside	185
XVIII	New Club / Picnic Interrupted	191
XIX	The Staff Cheers	201
XX	I Believe Her Story	207
XXI	Nannawanni Pie	215
	Acknowledgements	217

"I don't want to sit and wait for death---

I want to be part of the struggle of life!"

Anna Kreminetsky Trefman

A Different Mother

preface

"The life given to us is short but the memory of a life well spent is eternal." Cicero

Rena Trefman Cobrinik's book *A Different Mother* takes us through the transformation of the Jewish experience from early 1900s immigration in the Bronx, New York City, to post-war American citizenship in New Jersey. Although the storyline, reflecting a lifetime of challenges, may sound predictable and too personal to identify with, Cobrinik richly expands her characters, making them so familiar that only their names are foreign to us. The timeless ideals of respect, patience, and responsibility are sustained through each stage of life, from the innocence of youth to the callous ravages of old age.

Cobrinik's perspective on dementia and the devastating toll it exerts on loving, caring families, as well as patients, is particularly insightful and very instructive to me as a physician and, most important, for my medical students.

I have had the privilege of teaching medical students and residents at the Medical Humanities program at the Saint Barnabas Medical Center. The Medical Humanities discipline attempts to soften the hard, cold science curriculum with lectures in art, music, and literature and to ground future physicians in the understanding of the human condition. I invited Rena Cobrinik to speak to us on how we can be more conscious and acknowledge the enormously important role family members play in the care of our patients. A traditional arrogance of medicine with a focus solely on the scientific cause and effect often leads to a hopeless frustration and divide between physicians and family.

Cobrinik recalls her mother's revelation when, after multiple confusing hospitalizations and nursing home admissions, she is finally in a compassionate environment: "How great the people here are; they treat me as if I'm not sick. I never knew people could be so good."

Empathy is a very powerful skill that universally heals.

She has such a natural gift in her storytelling of complicated lives and events that resonate with each one of us as we progress through the series of regrets and optimistic expectations, trying to reach that understanding of the human condition. Cobrinik shares with us her greatest gift as a teacher.... learning to listen and respect one another.

John A. Russo, M.D.
St. Barnabas Medical Center

prologue

My mother, who was in love with life, seldom sent birthday cards to the children or me, but never missed sending them Valentine cards. I always wondered why. Then my son Zach emailed this story. I think the context reveals much about her approach to life.

As best as I could figure out, your mother's family spent virtually all of their money to purchase some sort of "cargo class" tickets on a ship that left Russia through the Black Sea and then the Mediterranean. Somewhere off the coast of Italy, there was a terrible storm, and all the men were called on deck to assist with the shifting cargo. As I understand it, your grandfather was severely injured during this process (probably crushed by something falling) and was put ashore in Italy (I think you believe it was Naples) as soon as possible and taken as quickly as possible (by ambulance?) to the hospital there. The rest of his family was told that he was going to something like "Municipal Hospital" and were left to find their own way there. No one in the family spoke Italian, and there were several "Municipal Hospitals" (or whatever the name they used was), so it took them a long time (I think a few days) to find the right place. By the time they did, their father was dead and their ship was gone, and they were in Italy with no money, no man and no ability to speak the language. I don't know a lot else, but I do know that at some point they were in Paris (see below), so it sounds as though they were wandering around Europe for a few years (I think the math works out to two years), trying to find a way to complete their journey to America. She told me about Paris one Valentine's Day.

> *"I was on a bus in Paris once when I was a young girl, when a man came onto the bus and walked right up to a woman next to me. Without a word, he put his arms around her and kissed her on the mouth and then walked away. I asked, 'Do you know him?' and she said, 'No, but it is Valentines Day, and on Valentines Day any man can kiss any woman without asking.' I had never heard of Valentines Day before, but I answered, 'That's a very nice holiday,' and I still think it is."*

She was grinning ear-to-ear as she told me this story that still made her smile after all these years. "When were you in Paris?" I asked. Her smile disappeared and her eyes became distant and misty. "I was there once, a long time ago, when I was still a young girl," she answered. "I was a lot of places," she added, her voice trailing off.

What she told me was simply, "Why not celebrate love?"

Anna with baby Rena, 1933

I

Elmhurst, Queens

My mother must have been in her forties. We were crossing the street, rushing...all dressed up, and we both had to slow down for an old bent wrinkled woman. My mother turned to me in the middle of the busy road, "So, do you think I'll be like that?" she asked.

"I hope so, Mom," I had answered, and we both laughed, racing between the cars. Neither of us could imagine her that way. I had hoped she would grow old and live a long happy life, but that vision left out a lot of details.

That was during World War Two; I was eleven or twelve. A ship had docked in New York Harbor. Sailors flooded the streets. I remember saying, "A sailor smiled at me."

"Yes, I saw," she said, "and at me too."

...Because she was my momma, I thought. Only now do I register that the pleasure in her face was not solely for me, a skinny little thing, delighted at being noticed, but was for the attention she received as well.

At the time I could never have imagined her walk becoming hesitant, her shoulders not thrust back, or her looking to me not so much with love as with relief for the tasks I would do for her.

As my mother grows old, she never thinks she may have to go to a nursing home. When her grandchildren visit, knowing she will die, she gives them her special pots, and tells them what and how to cook, so that they will be strong. She insists I take her favorite paintings and hang them in my house: an original colored lithograph that reminds her of her childhood home in Russia, a print of the prodigal son, whose message tempered her attitude towards her adult children, and a neighbor's large oil painting of a desert somewhere in the southwest. Finally, she gives me her tall and leafy plants. They had thrived, miraculously, in her studio apartment, which seldom gets any sun.

"I made a park for myself," she says. The plants camouflage the iron gate she had installed for protection after a sudden wave of robberies in her Queens middle-class building. The windows face the back alley.

I feel bad that my mother's last apartment has such a dismal setting. When I grew up in the Bronx, we lived on the top floor, and if you looked out of the window in my room, at a certain angle, you could see the George Washington Bridge and colorful sunsets. But my mother

2

insists she never misses that apartment. She moved into this last one after she left my father (and I, the youngest of three, had married). She saw it as a triumph: "This is only one room," she says, "but it's all mine." She often looks out at the buildings closing in and says, "See, I am never alone." Yet she doesn't know anyone behind those other windows well enough to talk to.

As always, her attitude becomes my own. I look out her window, her way: the alley becomes an enormous cement sculpture, a study in rectangles. Buildings jutting in and out at sharp angles accentuated by color, yellow brick, red, lines of black gates, airy boxes of fire-escapes against the high walls. Then rows of windows. Sometimes, a top row shines with a reflected light; the luminous glass lets you know the sun is shining. The windows sport shades, blinds and curtains of different colors. Birds dart back and forth, singing.

Her plants, verdant and lush, add life dispropor-tionate to the five strategically placed flower pots. Still, she wants me to have them. So even though I am sure they will die, I take them to my house, knowing that now she can hardly take care of herself.

Not only does she have trouble cooking and cleaning -- I have been coming by two or three times a week to help with that -- but dressing herself has become difficult. She barely remembers night or day or which family members are dead or alive. She phones me at all hours telling me she lost her key, or that someone has tampered with her door

3

lock, or that there is a man looking in her window. Often I respond as if she is only a little nervous. She might ask what time it is. Then, after I answer her, she asks, "...In the morning or at night?" If she hears me hesitate, she might add, "I took a nap so I'm not sure."

"And the man, Mom? Where is he standing?"

"On the ground."

"And you live on the third floor?"

"I don't need you to tell me I'm crazy," she snaps, the issue closed (I am no longer her confidante), and slams down the phone.

When I ask her to stay at my house for a few days, she refuses. She says that she feels better at her own house, that she knows where things are. An aide presented other difficulties. She didn't like a woman "over her head," even the nice one I'd hired who came in the mornings for about two months.

*   *   *

That year, before her final move to a nursing home, would prove to be the most difficult year in her hard life. During those last years, I would learn much about the difficulties of old age. And I would discover a different mother.

For six weeks in the spring, she had checked into Sunnyside Lodge, a nursing home not far from my house, recovering from a severe gastro-intestinal episode. Of course, she begged to leave: "I do not want to sit and wait for death. I want to be part of the struggle of life." I had noticed she had said "of life," not "for life."

A close friend of mine urges me to give in to my mother's wishes. "She will know when she can no longer manage. I only wish that I had given my mother another year before we insisted that she go to a home," my friend says.

And she helps me settle my mother back in her apartment. My friend shops and stocks the refrigerator while I unpack my mother's suitcases and get the air-conditioning going. My friend is a great comfort, walking into the building with us, past the neighbors in the hall, and while we wait for the elevator she is even more comforting.

I have begun to absorb my mother's fear that the management is trying to oust her from the building. There is a lot of condo activity -- pressure to buy. The tenants are organizing meetings and circulating petitions. The elevators vibrate with the issue. I understand the source of her fears, and know that the elderly cannot be forced to buy, but I worry that her new frailties combined with her old belligerence might not win the management's sympathy. I am wrong.

It has been a record hot summer. Newspapers warn us that this heat is the beginning of global warming. People -- squinting, despite their baseball caps or straw hats -- stand in front of the building's entrance enduring the heat, avoiding the isolation and confinement of their air-conditioned apartments. They stand like mannequins, dulled by the breezeless air and the oppressive sun; fumes of melting tar anesthetize them as well. Yet as soon as they see us, they reach out, smiling,

"Anna, you look well."

"How are you?"

"So good to see you."

The welcome is high-spirited; all that is missing is the band. They seem buoyed that she is strong enough to return. She acknowledges them, her manner cool, like an entitled dignitary accustomed to a grand entrance. I feel hopeful that she will manage.

Once she is settled, I learn that the superintendent, a Caribbean, who, I sense, does not approve of my leaving her alone, urges my mother to sit in front of the building "so she wouldn't be lonely." The other tenants are discouraged from sitting there since the building is going condo and they want to attract the "right people."

As usual, neighbors going and coming greet her, and she is still aware of and included in their intrigues. Ben, her biggest fan, a burly retired fireman in his seventies, has lost his wife to cancer a few years before. My mother has told me how he asks her for advice about his affairs, and how they laugh at their children's presumptions that their lives are over. Of course my mother then laughs at his quest for eternal youth. "All he wants is for his schmuck to stand," she says.

Three-year-old Nancy from next door races up to my mother and kisses her on her wizened cheek.

"So?" she says, as the little girl stands waiting, "What about the other cheek?" And right on cue, Nancy leans over and kisses the other cheek. Sometimes she runs back to her mother, loaded with bundles, who may wave or make light conversation, but this evening rushes to teach a course at the community college not far away. My role has been established: I am only to nod politely.

Often, after a visit, I leave my mother sitting there on her aluminum beach chair in the evening dusk. I watch the passing procession with her for a while: a tall dark man with a high elegant turban; a short stocky woman wearing a flowing pink sari; two teenage boys chasing each other; dogs on leashes held by pretty girls; a sedate Asian grandfather, in a three piece suit, walking his rambunctious grandson; fat women; old men; cars and trucks passing; a screaming ambulance.

"See, do I need television with a show like this?" she asks. While the street provides life size drama, the truth is that she has not learned how to work her new TV's remote control.

"This is life before me, not like your house, stuck in the woods, the trees standing like silent witnesses." She says that often, defending her decision and her authority. Although I know she really is happier in her neighborhood, I am still worried. I know people on the city streets are not watching out for her interests, and I also know how very fragile her heart is.

One evening I cannot reach my mother by phone. I

am sure that she has died, and I call one of her neighbors. She looks for her and finds her outside in front of the house, sitting and chatting. She calls me back, "Let your mother die as she wishes; let death find her."

II

Old Times

"Only Renale I can't leave," Shoshana cried as she leaned against the ship's railing, her thick braids falling forward. I was in my mother's arms, waving to the people in the boat. "Only Renale I can't leave." These were the last words Shoshana, then thirteen years old, had spoken in America. I was only two years old. Our family had gone to see the Greenbergs off to Palestine, though I never understood why they left.

They had lived next door to our family in a Bronx apartment building. Shoshana, their daughter, played house or school with my sister and brother while her parents taught at the Hebrew Seminary. Everyone, even the children, spoke Yiddish then: my sister Bernice, my brother Simon, and Shoshana, who was five years older than Bernice. That is, they spoke Yiddish until my brother and sister started school, when a social worker came to our apartment and told my parents not to speak Yiddish to us. "You're in America, now," she said.

I would not meet the Greenbergs again until I was an adult, but I would hear their stories many times; I knew Shoshana's words as well as lyrics in a popular song. Her photos, a girl with those thick long braids and broad smile, spilled out of books, but to me she could have been Rapunzel. Portraits of her parents, Monya and Baruch, I'd discovered buried in boxes, and I had to ask who those old fashioned people stiffly posed on a photographer's bench were. But the departure story was so familiar that I would recognize us on the screen as I watched departures in old movies, with Humphrey Bogart or Fred Astaire. We were there, and somehow it was always summer.

Monya Greenberg had grown up with my father in a small city in the Ukraine. She married Baruch there. My parents met and married in America. Once the couples found each other, they became good friends -- my parents and the Greenbergs -- visiting each other across the hall, back and forth, as comfortable in one kitchen as the other.

I understand that Baruch had a role in choosing my name. At the time, Bialik, the famous Palestinian poet, was a friend of Baruch's. He had come to America to watch the bicycle races. My mother told me that the three men had named me: my father, Bialik, and Baruch.

"They stayed up all night and chose the name 'Rena,' because on the morning you were born," she said, "the Saturday's Torah portion was *'Rena V Simcha'* . . . a joyful song," (the joy after the sorrow, marking the end of *Tisha b'Ov*, a somber holiday memorializing the destruction of the second temple in Jerusalem).

For me it was always hard to reconcile my parents' association with literary people and their almost desperate struggle to get "food on the table and clothes on our backs." I'd heard about dessert with Bialik at the Greenbergs. My mother said she was late for the dessert because she had to put her children, my brother and sister, to bed. She did not let the honored guest's presence eclipse hers.

At first, after the Greenbergs left for Palestine, there was little contact between the families. My mother used to say, "What will I write? If I write good news they will think I'm bragging, and if I write bad news they will think I'm begging." But she talked about them in hushed, subdued tones . . . implying that she may have had a role in their leaving, even taking the blame for their departure. She never said more. It was not her style to leave a statement so bare, not to embellish it in some way by explanation or often dramatization. And though I did not pursue it, I was unaware for a long time that her rare restraint had made its own impression.

Mostly she told stories reliving the good times -- intimate stories, describing Shoshana and my grandmother or Monya's relationship with her domestic help; "She made her polish the stove with shoe polish!" was one of many digs my mother repeated to ridicule and discredit Monya every

11

so often, even going so far as to report on Monya's sexual indiscretions.

A story my mother repeated often, and that I thought quite remarkable, described an incident that occurred when I was about eighteen months old. I had been in the Greenberg's apartment on a Sunday morning. Baruch was still in bed. I pulled and pulled at his hand. Finally, he followed me until I led him back to my family's apartment where I seated myself on the potty.

"You are smarter than me, Renale. Without saying a word you knew what to do; you are smarter than me," he had said.

My mother would quote his words, as proudly as if it were a Valedictory speech; I'd be embarrassed, surprised that anything as simple, as ordinary, and as private would be recounted with so much pleasure, particularly since bodily functions were not otherwise mentioned when I was growing up. Baruch's casual attitude, especially for a man of his generation and culture, made an impression on me. I did not understand why he appreciated my "achievement" so. Even more incomprehensible was how often my mother repeated the story.

Almost twenty years after the Greenbergs had left America, a year after I graduated from college, not quite twenty-two years old, I visited them in Israel. I had gone to Rome (with money earned from my first teaching job), and then, out of the blue, I received a letter from Baruch inviting me to visit them in Israel. More remarkable, once there I felt totally at ease with these story-tale people.

By then, Shoshana was the mother of two little girls. I shared my mother's stories with her.

"Your mother was so important to me," Shoshana said, as we sat in her Jerusalem kitchen. Curtains my mother made for her hung on the windows: black and yellow flowered print. "Do they really use such colors for curtains in America?"

I shrugged. They didn't.

"Yes, she was special," she continued looking past me to the curtains, as if the flowers were blooming in moonlight. "Once I was sitting in the lobby of our building, waiting for my parents to come home from work. Your mother walked by just as the superintendent was chasing me out. 'Look here,' she said, 'you can't speak to her like that. She is a young lady . . . .'"

"'. . . You must ask her politely,'" I completed the story.

Shoshana smiled, and told another, "I was just beginning to develop physically and was unsure -- you know. Your mother said, 'Don't worry Shoshanale, some breasts are apples and others are pears . . . ,'" I nodded, ready for the familiar line, "'. . . all fruit is beautiful.'"

After that visit, Shoshana and I kept in touch with intense but sporadic contact.

My mother left my father soon after I married, and a few years later both my father and Baruch would die. That my mother and Shoshana also corresponded, I learned only by accident. I had come across a letter that lay open on my mother's dresser. Shoshana had written that she appreciated my mother's consolation regarding Monya's death, since others had dismissed Shoshana's grief, because Monya, at least ninety, was so old when she died.

Once Shoshana heard that my mother was not well, she wrote to her: "No one else could know how unique and wonderful that time had been, when the two families had been so close."

But I knew the stories of that closeness, often revealed in a code of smiles and sighs.

*   *   *

Much later, after my mother died, clearing a space for a new computer, I had to remove her black pocketbook, which had been resting on the shelf for almost a year. This time I combed it thoroughly. As calm as I'd been about her death, that was something I had not been able to do. I found a picture of my family at my younger son David's Bar Mitzvah, and, from my sister, Bernice who lives in California, a note card where she'd written that she thought of my mother often. There was also an old plastic bankbook case. I dug around in it and found a folded piece of lined paper that had been torn out of a spiral notebook, folded till it was about only an inch square: a note to Shoshana.

My mother's handwriting, Cyrillic letters forming English words, always seemed to me like a visual accent left over from her Russian schooling, where she had completed

Gymnasium. The usual graceful curves of that alphabet
were scrawled and shaky. The words were not straight on
the lines, and the salutation and signature were written in
Yiddish. She had written the letter, I realized, at her
second visit to Sunnyside Lodge, the local nursing home.

In the letter, she wrote that suddenly her life came
back to her, and that she cried to know where she was. (She
had never cried or complained to me.) She thanked
Shoshana for a picture she had sent of my sister and
Shoshana together in California, and added, "Rena was only
2 years old. She did not know a thing about the closeness of
the family. I framed the picture. I do not know how long
I'll look at you." (I have never seen this photo.)

"The closeness, the closeness," I had heard so much
about it; I had even seen it. When my mother was at
Sunnyside Lodge recuperating from her gastro-enteritis,
Shoshana, on her way to a family wedding, stopped to visit
us in New Jersey. She wanted to see my mother. So I
brought her to my house for the day, from the Lodge. I was
busy getting things for lunch, and the two of them sat
together and talked. I had not seen Shoshana and my
mother together before, but both had told me about their
love for each other. Their closeness that day had a
mysterious quality -- the two of them sitting on the deck,
surrounded by trees so heavy with foliage there was no
visible sky. It seemed as if the present, the day, the light
were blocked out. Even Shoshana seemed comfortably
rooted in the past, as if my mother's voice physically

connected her to memories, rather than to the conversation they were having. The words seemed unimportant, only the closeness.

I felt as if I had no place there.

Later that day, when I drove Shoshana back to the city, she talked excitedly about the families, how wonderful that time had been, ". . . And your mother was such a big part of . . . ," and then she held back. Perhaps I was afraid to press for more information. But the stories now feel incomplete.

My mother once said that she lost contact with most of her friends during the Depression. I wasn't sure if it was because of her pride or if it was, as she'd often said, "People don't bother with you when you're low."

My mother was unwilling to discuss the matter; she would either change the subject or find an errand for me to do. Possibly it was the change of our family fortunes that my mother didn't want to embroider; she didn't like to ruminate about her misfortunes. I had heard we'd been prosperous. My father had once owned three bookstores and had traded rare books. Once the Depression hit, bought books were a luxury; people went to libraries. So we kept moving east, to places in the Bronx where the living was cheaper.

The bad luck was not limited to the struggle with poverty: my mother's arm had been smashed in a car accident. She was one of the first people to have a bone grafted from her leg to her arm. In a body cast for a year and a half, she seldom talked about it, as if there were some shame surrounding the accident. She could not speak because of her enormous guilt -- because of how we kids suffered. We had been shunted from orphanages to relatives and friends. Afterward, to discharge that guilt, like the Ancient Mariner, she'd tell me over and over about my brother's nightmares after his stay in a children's home, and how he said no one there was as pretty as his momma.

I must have been three, and I remember being bathed by others in different homes. In one, I felt like a burden, a charity case, a product of an incompetent and inferior world -- my mother's. At the home of my mother's friend Sophie, who bathed me in a kitchen tub, I felt treasured. She would say how she loved bathing me, since she had only boys. Later, when my brother had had a mastoid and infantile paralysis, I stayed at my Aunt Jenny's house; it smelled of oatmeal cookies even in the bathtub -- that tub had no feet and was surrounded by glistening white tiles. I also remembered my time with the Liebs, distant cousins, where I felt enveloped with love, though my mother had seldom mentioned them.

When I try to think back to that early time, the houses I stayed at and my family's house blend into one. How small and crowded the first apartment was! But at the time I did not realize it; I knew only that I was finally with my family. Happy. And we had a piano in the kitchen. My

17

sister, Bernice played "There Is a Tavern in the Town," Gilbert and Sullivan operettas, and Mozart. Something was always cooking on the stove: stuffed cabbage simmering, brisket, tongue, potato cakes, a wonderful soup made from yellow pike (I am still looking for the recipe), steaks, lamb chops, even spaghetti.

Besides the big kitchen, the next room, railroad-flat-style, with no hallways to separate it, contained only a studio-couch and a single bed. Bernice had the bed to herself; my brother Simon and my father shared the studio, with separate bedding. I did not question the sleeping arrangements. No, my mother would not put my brother and sister together as other parents did. Nor, her logic went, could my sister and I sleep together. I was too little, fragile; she would crush me. So I slept with my mother in the tiny back room. Sometimes my mother's leg would hold me tight, or, when she turned over, I would lean against the cool wall. I was with my mother again, like a baby kangaroo.

Often when I went to bed my father would lie down next to me and tell me about the adventures of Gunther Cossack, a Russian giant. He lay down next to me, yet I do not know if my parents found time for each other in that bed, although I sensed no discord between them; they seemed to get on well then. My mother had survived the operation from that terrible accident which had dismembered our young lives as well, and she was exuberant about being able to work with that arm.

My father was always looking for work, but his knowledge of the classics could not help put food on the table. Yet when he found a business opportunity in Connecticut, he deferred to my mother, and did not move us away from her family in the Bronx. She appreciated that; in later years she often commented on his generosity, his sacrifice.

Soon times got better for us. The war started. My mother went to work in a factory, sewing pilots' insulated uniforms; my father started a business importing cheap Chinese fur for mittens and slippers. We moved to a larger apartment in the west Bronx. Now that I was older, my sister Bernice and I shared a room. The piano and a few fine pieces of Baker furniture stood in the living room, where my brother slept on the studio couch covered with a new wide-grain corduroy slipcover. There were bookcases and lamp lights. And my parents were together in a room of their own. Possibly the long separations and the odd sleeping arrangements evened out.

Once we moved, my Saturdays included piano lessons and cleaning the apartment with my mother. I also often helped prepare dinner with her when she came back so tired from her factory job. By the time I was eleven, during summer vacations, I'd run the house -- making beds and starting dinner. I felt an enormous sense of peace, creating a calm orderly home. My mother appreciated my efforts, but did not demand them, or even expect them. She did not want me to feel burdened by her work. When my aunt said

19

she thought we children should do more, she'd respond with a question, "Who gives your children breakfast?"

Much of what I knew about my family depended as much on stories as on experience. Sometimes the story was brief. All my father volunteered was, "My mother was very pious." I pushed for more: "But did you have brothers, sisters?" Only one word: *"Derharget!"* Murdered.

During the hard times, our house was noisy and filled with people, but they were mostly neighbors, people who were not part of our history. To learn about my family (or my parents' earlier life), stories substituted for visits; the people in them were alive -- real, and I learned that their value was proportionate to how long and how often the stories were told. The Greenbergs in Palestine were brought up often; their name resonated in our kitchen. The Liebs, who lived nearby, only seemed to get a footnote.

III

Visit to Becky Lieb

"Hurry, hurry, after all she's ninety-two." She's talking about a visit to Becky Lieb, whom, except for a Bar Mitzvah I'd gone to after my honeymoon, I haven't seen in fifty years. On that occasion I barely spoke to anyone; I was still too starry-eyed. When we got home, my husband asked about Becky Lieb and her husband, who looked at me, he said, "with so much love."

"Distant cousins," I had said, knowing they were a social casualty to the Depression.

As unexpected as my mother's request is, when she asks me to take her to Becky Lieb's, I think, "What a lovely idea!" and never question why. At the same time I find myself resisting my mother. Her urgency, her intensity, make me feel as if she is pulling me onto a magnetic track zigzagging this way and that. I try to put it off until after I go to my periodontist, or after a visit to her doctor -- her blood pressure has to be monitored.

"Hurry, hurry . . . ," she says. I begin to judge just how necessary each request is and do not automatically follow her orders on my visiting days, as I may have before when her requests were more logical and less voluminous.

"After all, Rena, she's ninety-two; we have to hurry."

"Sure, Mom, I have only good feelings." I really would like to see Becky Lieb. Finding her however, becomes another project; but finally, after some detective work, I call Franny, Becky's youngest daughter, whom I haven't seen in fifty years.

"Hello," I say, "this is Rena . . . ." Before I can finish the sentence, Franny interrupts; her voice sounds familiar and warm.

"Rena, darling, my God, you bring back the excitement we felt at having a baby in the house," she says.

I had stayed at the Liebs' after my mother's arm had been broken. I remembered lovingly my time with the Liebs.

Now, Becky Lieb lives in a twelve-story red brick apartment house in Riverdale, a suburb of the Bronx. The building houses former city employees and union members. Becky's husband had been a window washer, and my mother says he was a smart, sociable man and a credit to the building, which has a very nice class of people.

We ring the bell, are buzzed in, and go up in the elevator. As soon as I open its door, I see Becky waiting at the end of the hall by the open door of her apartment. We stand there holding on to our open doors: I, waiting for my mother to walk out, she, waiting for us. She looks exactly as I remember her. Her eyes are dark, almond shaped, almost Chinese. Her hair has less gray than mine. We hug and hug.

"Renale, Renale." Little Rena she calls me, though I now tower over her. I see the lines on her face and notice how wobbly her bowed legs are.

We enter a sparkling apartment. Photographs cover the walls and surfaces; glossy images of the last fifty years are everywhere. Framed collections of weddings and Bar Mitzvahs, single pictures of new babies and great grandchildren share surfaces with her myriad of plants. There must be thirty or forty, in plastic pots, clay pots, decorated porcelain pots of all sizes and colors. In each pot there are thin sticks, like chopsticks, standing in the soil, their tops covered with red or bright blue hand crocheted booties about an inch long -- possibly Becky's way to add the color of flowers.

"See how beautiful Becky keeps everything," my mother says.

"I'll show you everything, but first let's eat," Becky says.

I had brought some coffee cake.

"No, you will have to take it home. I have everything."

23

I had offered to take the women out, but Becky had insisted on preparing the lunch.

"What is it? I'll make a little tuna fish . . . and . . . ." she said when I had called.

Sure enough the tuna fish and accoutrements -- cantaloupe already cut, tomatoes sliced -- are set out on the table, which we share with about ten plants, booties and all.

"See," she says, "nothing is out, but everything is here." And indeed, everything was organized for our visit, even the white bread stands waiting in the toaster.

Once we sit down, the women look at each other.

"It's Stanley's *yahrtzeit*," Becky tells us -- the first year anniversary of her son's death. My brother died four years earlier. The women look at each other, their eyes fill with tears; fingers quiver on the table. Then Becky, her voice hoarse with pain, tells us what happened.

"He didn't feel good one night. I wanted to see him," Becky says. "But he said, 'It's the grippe, Mom, wait till I'm over it,' and then the next day he died." The last phrase is in Yiddish. My mother repeats it.

"Un er's geshtarben." And then he died. She can't share her story: my brother's three agonizing months with kidney cancer. The women look at each other over the brightly booteed plants, their eyes fill and they do not speak.

I cannot sit there so I start washing the cantaloupe dishes. I still feel the pain of my brother's death, but leave them alone. Both have lost a child, their only sons -- a terrible loss, and not in the natural order of life, which adds to their suffering.

As soon as she realizes I am at her sink, Becky practically jumps up and then whips out a towel hanging inside a cabinet.

"See, I have everything in place," she says, and dismisses me.

She conducts a tour of her three-room-apartment as proudly as if she lives in a DuPont mansion, pointing out the lampshades she had made for the lamps flanking her bed: champagne silk in a pagoda style, their narrow three inch-diameter on top widening out in a beautifully crafted graceful flare, with not a speck of dust on their fine scalloped welted edges -- not after thirty years in a New York apartment. My mother, who is at best a casual housekeeper, repeats, "See, how nice Becky keeps everything."

Becky, possibly responding to the praise, opens her closets, pointing out how orderly everything is, how easy the suitcases are to get at if she were going on a trip. As it happens, she confides that her last trip had been to a nursing home after her hip operation. A young woman there, who was writing a report, had asked the residents to tell about themselves. Becky told how she came to stay in America. I ask Becky to tell us the story; my mother leans back on the green velvet couch and listens.

"It was only for a visit. I was fifteen and visiting my brothers in America. It was 1913. When I was ready to go

back to Russia the war started. So what was I to do?"
Becky paused before revealing her strategy for survival.

"I wrapped my three braids around my head with two
pounds of hairpins and I looked like a mensch, a person."
My mother nods as Becky smiles with satisfaction, as if she
had just pinned her hair up that morning. I remember her
thick black braids wound around her head; yes, I remember
that from the back her head looked like a Victorian
footstool.

As Becky describes herself as a young girl I look at
my mother, who has come without her lower teeth, which
were being adjusted for her shrinking gums. I thought
she'd put off the visit until they were ready. She was
usually quite particular about her appearance. "It is not
important," she had said. Now she smiles too, her lower lip
drawn in to cover her gums.

Becky continues, "So then I got a job in a box factory,
and then another, and I met Saul and here I am." She looks
at my mother, "You remember, Chana?"

My mother nods, and does not correct her and say,
"Call me Anna," as she usually demands of other relatives.

In fact my mother adds what she knows to Becky's
story: that Saul, an orphan, had lived with her family for a
few years in Russia. The women go over details, such as
which town Saul had come from, and trace how my mother
and he are cousins. It is convoluted but they both agree.

As visits go, I am surprised at how quiet my mother
is -- and how agreeable. Yet the years have not been

bridged: jokes are missing, though Becky seems satisfied that she has brought us up to date with the family news; we've handled each framed photo.

The three of us are seated on the couch. Becky turns to me and says, "You know, Mother said you had to have bacon." She pauses and slowly turns her head and shoulders and shoots an accusing look at my mother, who, although she is sitting erect, does not respond. She is not listening as before, when Becky related her American adventure; this time my mother seems preoccupied with her own memories. Her eyes are clearly focused, but not on us.

Becky turns back to me, her eyes confiding, her voice reciting; a separate manner for each of us.

"I was kosher," she says, "so I sent you to Mrs. Kelly."

"Because I was so thin," I say, to defend my mother, as I always do.

"Yeah, you were thin," Becky says. "I made you a birthday party when you were four years old. Remember? I invited all the children."

I can't remember. Then I look toward my mother for confirmation. She looks straight at me, and this time, her expression is blank.

Becky Lieb continues. "Sadie, she should rest in peace, said she wasn't getting tied down with a baby. I told her, 'I have three, I'll have four. I'll take Rena.' You missed your mother, and one day said to me, 'Becky, I know my mother is sick; maybe if I go home I can take care of her and make her well.' You said that."

27

"How long was I with you?"

"It was five and a half months."

Five months. I never thought about it that way --
just little blots, like Sunday afternoon visits -- Saul's face
smiling, and Mildred, Stanley, and Franny, too.

She goes on describing the visit and my life in ways I
have not heard before, how she loved hearing me say a
Yiddish phrase, "You said you'd *chup up*' the food," eat it
quickly. Then she stands up and imitates me cleaning a
scuff mark off a pair of white sandals she'd bought me. She
licks her finger with spit, bends down over her bowed legs
and rubs an imaginary spot on her black heavy serviceable
shoes. I had rarely heard myself described as a baby, or
heard my childish ways cherished.

I always knew there were enough other things going
on in my mother's life, what with her factory job, my
brother's illnesses, her struggle with poverty -- making up
for my father's surrender to it with what I now understand
to be a deep depression, a lot of sleeping. Sometimes she'd
sew pretty dresses for me or make wonderful blintzes. I
was happy enough just to be with her. Still, Becky's talk
seems, to me, like a nice dessert.

But as Becky carries the photograph albums for us to
look at, I decide we have to go. I want to beat the traffic, it
being Friday on a Labor Day weekend. At the same time, I
assure her that it is an easy ride from Queens and that we
will come again. My mother stands without a word and is
ready to go. I have the feeling she is pleased with the visit

and was not concerned with Becky's remark about the bacon.

Becky insists on coming down and showing us the building's backyard. My mother says, sure, she wants to see it. We walk down the wide cement steps in a line, holding on to the pipe that serves as a banister. My mother is moving like she's performing a part in a play. She is erect and seems to look out to the audience; as if they are seated at the cement tables where Saul used to play cards. But today there are no people. My mother whispers that if Saul were alive, people would be there. "He was very sociable. He was the sociable one," she says.

The women gossip about children married and grown, how Ida was the only woman to play cards. It is all well and good, but I am getting more concerned about traffic. Finally, after I help my mother into the car, I stand on the sidewalk to say good-bye to Becky.

"I hug you," she says, "but I feel only Renale. You know your mother left you by me a lot. She would say she had to go shopping and then go home and clean up the apartment. I did not mind. They warned me about what your mother was doing," Becky says, a little louder now, and tilts her head toward my mother in the car, "but I didn't mind watching you," she adds. Then Becky Lieb turns and faces my mother, who was already seated in the car. She leans forward and says, "I forgive you for that."

"And I forgive you too. Don't you remember the good

things? Can't you remember them?" My mother's voice is firm.

"I forgive you. I forgive you for making me give her bacon."

"And I forgive you for what you are saying." That is the last thing my mother says, and then she looks toward the road, her head high, as if she lifted it away from the stench of the argument to consider a purchase, something mundane – shoes, or merely a pair of stockings.

I hug Becky tightly and walk to the driver's seat. From the corner of my eye, I think I see a shadow of hawk's wings, a piece of my childhood in its claws. Seated at the driver's wheel, I welcome the weekend traffic which I hope will distract me from my clashing emotions -- my gratitude for what Becky had done for me so long ago, and sadness because of her betrayal, her unexpected outburst, her attack on my mother.

With my mother, the champion slugger, arguments could materialize out of the simplest comments, but this time it seemed my mother had come to apologize; the visit alone indicated that. But she had miscalculated Becky's anger. Becky had played it cool, sized up the situation, and then, after all those years, swung back--with all the vigor of a tennis player returning a difficult serve--ending the game.

* * *

On the drive home neither my mother nor I speak, though we are not quiet people. I kiss my mother and I let her off.

"Well, I won't go again," she finally says.

I call her when I get home. "No, the traffic wasn't bad," I say. Then add, "Too bad, Mom, that Becky had to say all that."

"Who heard it? After all she's ninety-two. If she knew how to add it would be only eighty-eight. It was Ida who left her son with her. She left him when she played cards. What does it matter? She could only brag about her life, how good she was and clean. She was a maid. She left that out."

Before preparing dinner, I take a shower to wash away the long afternoon, the traffic, the actual physical demands of the day, and its more elusive innuendoes.

Becky's love washes over me as I try to sort my thoughts. Even if she had scores of her own to settle, even if my mother were right and Becky Lieb had got it wrong, even if my mother could not admit how bad times were, shouldn't I have known that Becky took care of me for five and one-half months?

There must be more that I should know as well. Why would my mother risk going to Becky without her bottom teeth? What had happened so long ago that made the visit end so disastrously?

"They warned me about what you were doing." Becky's sweet lips soured as she spat the words at my mother and her good intentions. The women had looked only at each other, past me, through me. What terrible

31

thing could my mother have done to keep Becky so angry for over fifty years?

The soap slips through my hands. Once I return it to its dish, I rinse myself, step out of the shower stall and wrap myself in a towel. Something happened, I think, patting myself dry. What had she done?

IV

Contradictions

It is almost nine months since our visit to Becky Lieb. I knock at the door, then let myself in with my key and call out, "Ma, hello . . . hello," to the empty but lighted rooms.

My mother, who was probably in the bathroom, styling her hair, walks briskly across the living room; the comb strokes are visible in the damp wave falling across her forehead as she enters the quiet kitchen without a word. Then she stands still and silently looks me over.

I feel her examine my clothes, my hair, and am gratefully distracted by the bunch of freshly washed beets on the sink's white porcelain counter -- water shimmering on threads of their round bulbous roots. I think of the borscht, the sweet cold soup they will become, and pointing to them say, "Mom, let's make it now . . . ."

She looks at the beets, then at me, and shakes her head, "You will come and sit with me and cook?

"No good," she says.

I know she refuses to cook with me because she doesn't want to be dependent on me. "No good." I'd heard it before.

In the past it could have been be a sharp rebuke or a physical assault. A comb would appear, my chin none too gently placed at an angle, and a vigorous restyling would be set in motion. My husband would eye the results, horrified.

She is sizing up more than my looks. Her disapproval feels as familiar to me as the pillow I lay my head on each night. "No good." She'd wear it like a badge, deriding any soft, marshmallow-like accommodations I might express. Now I feel it in her glance. I believe she wants me to know that she is still strong, even hard.

She would not deny meanness.

"I remember the first time I was mean," she said, and actually licked her lips as she relished the story she was about to tell.

"I was a little girl, and was walking to school with another girl from the *shtetl*, the town. She was rich, and wore red ribbons in her hair. She walked ahead of me all *farpitzed*, all gussied up. Her ribbon slipped off her braid onto the ground." My mother would always pause here, "Then, with my toe, I pushed the ribbon in the mud." And she would look down at the floor and delicately point her toe, gently dancing an imaginary ribbon into the mud, then purse her lips in satisfaction.

She would not deny meanness, yet she wanted me to be a good girl and a good woman as well. Now, all grown-up, I can't believe we are standing in this still kitchen, replaying old battles. I think how different this hush is from the lively theatrics we used to have -- at the end, we'd laugh them away: "Now shall we play Act 2?" one of us might have asked, when we'd gotten a little too hot.

The "no goods" let up when I became an elementary school teacher. She seemed satisfied, even proud. For a year, I worked in an all-boy ghetto school where urine in the halls, and desks thrown out of the windows were everyday events. After a long tired day, if I said anything flippant about my students, she'd say, "You can make a difference, change their lives, they are poor children," until the time I had forgotten my classroom keys. She brought them to the school, and, after walking through halls covered with obscene graffiti, heavy with pungent odors -- and, she later confided, the tension of rape in the air -- she feared for my life. "Don't go back!" she said, and was angry when I did.

Her messages were always a well of contradictions. I was used to them. She'd had a pretty mixed up childhood, demands steeped in contradictions. The cigarette story made that clear.

Her father had a bad heart; he smoked and knew that he had to stop. She was just a little girl and he would ask her to hide his cigarettes. Under no circumstances was she to tell him where she hid them. He would beat her if she did. Then she would add the story's catch, "But then he would ask for the cigarettes, and I would not tell," she'd say, and pause -- with that smug satisfaction of one who has kept her word -- and then . . . "So he beat me. But I *still* wouldn't tell."

The story was always told with bravado -- nor did she ever accuse her father. She'd laugh . . . still proud that she had not revealed the hiding place. For her this was not a no-win story. She could take it. No man intimidated her!

I remember the time she bargained for a trunk I needed for summer-camp. The bargaining became intense, I was ready to send my clothes in a cardboard carton, or stay home for the summer.

"It's garbage," she said to the salesman. "What do you take me for? . . . to spend twelve dollars on that?"

"Ma, don't Ma . . . , " I remember begging.

"Be quiet," she said, with no pause in her haggling. When we left the store with the trunk at her price, she admonished me to never interrupt a bargaining maneuver, no matter what she might toss at the salesperson.

"Take it," she said. "He can and you can too." She was proud of being able to dish it out.

Yet with all her "no goods" and "do betters," I've always known that there is nothing contradictory about her love for me. But I also know that she is disappointed with the way I've turned out. My choice not to pursue a profession or to go on for an advanced degree remains a major quarrel between us.

When I was a child, she encouraged me to be a union organizer. Her union had begun to train their own and she would have loved me to take part in its program. Once, at dinner, between lamb chops and Jell-O, glorifying my mission, she described a melee in the South, rhapsodizing about a young woman, "a beautiful redhead," who got bashed in the head while trying to improve the lives of southern workers. It was clear that, for the workers, the young organizer was their salvation; but when I looked at it from my own angle (not willing to be a casualty for the cause), my mother lost her case.

I laugh whenever I tell that story, but its subscript was no joke. I took it as a warning not to be carried away by her passion and to look out for my own head.

I was used to her talent for holding opposite views simultaneously: night and day existed together in her sky. But her desire, passionately expressed, that I have a profession, held no contradictions. She'd encourage any possibility, union organizer or school-teacher. She'd campaign relentlessly. Any occasion, an Arthur Miller drama or the neighborhood gossip, would serve her "and you see . . ." lessons. The tragedy of Miller's protagonist in *Death of a Salesman* had an obvious explanation: "And you see what happens without a college education," she'd say. "A woman needs a profession, regardless of her husband's salary." But this view was not necessarily accepted by others.

Long before Betty Friedan's book, I remember telling a girl at school that I wanted to be a teacher, citing advantages, such as the hours, which would not interfere with family life, and, in case of an ill or philandering husband, I could carry the load. And then added, what was most important, "I'd have a life of my own." As soon as those last five words were spoken, the girl's reaction surprised me so, that I can still see the scene. I can feel the stony dampness of the gym's cement floor and the height of the peach-colored gates on the gym windows. I can hear her whispered response, "A woman must live for her family." The girl could be standing before me. I see her long neck, her green narrow eyes, her flared skirt and her silent movement away from me.

It seemed as if I would have to navigate through my mother's contradictions at home or away.

By the time I got to high school, my friends would visit our house to hear my mother's stories about Isadora Duncan or Emma Goldman -- daring, passionate women. While my mother admired those qualities, she warned us not to be taken with those women: they were also crazy and frivolous. For her it was that simple. Even when she chose the subject, contradictory messages were tossed out with certainty and conviction. But by then I was not uncomfortable with them. I took what I needed from each.

Once I married, in my early twenties, I began to question her expectations. Released from the seductive smells of soups and pies, plates crowded with blintzes, I began to see her part in my parents' unsuccessful marriage.

My father seldom spoke, and only later did I understand that he was never given the opportunity: the family was her show, a one-woman performance. During my childhood, I saw only her side, and agreed that he could do nothing right.

One afternoon, friends were at the house, we were in the living room and my father, standing near the bookcase, said that the Hudson River in New York City was a salt-water river. I laughed at him too. I rolled on the couch. Any ten year old knew that rivers were sweet-water, and oceans were salt. His point that rivers close to the ocean had salt-water fish barely got a hearing. He smiled, acknowledging that I was right generally. He struggled, tapping his pipe on his palm, desperately trying to explain (between his difficulties with the language and the actual effort to be listened to). Much later I would learn that certain salt-water fish were swimming in the Hudson River, an estuary, where the river meets the sea.

Though he seldom spoke, there were occasions when he exploded with pent up anger and rage. I remember vividly ludicrous accusations about my mother and other men, what appeared to be his fantasies about a love life they did not share. I barely heard his words, "the way she runs around," swallowed in a cough. Amazingly, she did not defend herself.

I planned to succeed in my marriage, which she had heartily approved of and then wanted to save me from. During the time I was unhappy and considered a divorce,

she fought me. She brought up issues of loyalty and
dependence, disregarding her on-going campaigns for
independence and strength.

Heady with youth, swept into a different world, I
learned to go my own way. She accepted my move to the
suburbs, though she did not endorse it. There, I taught
third grade while cows grazed in a meadow adjoining the
playground. I enjoyed both a pastoral idyll and a
profession. I founded the school newspaper, organized a
community clothing drive for Hungarian refugees, and
heard no disapproval from my mother.

But when I had a baby, and chose to stay home to
care for her and the two others that followed, her
disapproval was blunt. Like octopus ink, it colored
everything I did: my cooking ("the meat was dry"), my
decorating ("the lamp stands like a fat cow"), my house ("too
many windows"), and my clothes ("no sense of style"). To
underscore my lack of savvy, she also complained that I
didn't drink or serve good wine. But I was so taken with my
life I hardly heard her. As dull as it may have appeared to
her, I was happily consumed by it, grateful for the luxury of
caring for my kids -- free from her maelstrom. I worked on
a committee to improve education in my town, organized
book drives for desegregated schools, and managed married
life (possibly the most challenging job of all).

During those years, she sounded like Phillip Roth's
Mrs. Portnoy: "'Get an office of your own.' Start a doctorate
in psychology. A maid can take care of the children and

house." My choice did not fulfill her dream that I be a sophisticated professional woman, who dressed stylishly and moved quickly. That's how, given the opportunity, she would have done it.

Later, when the children were in high school, I did find a job as an insurance adjuster and investigator -- a job which at that time was rare for women. But no matter what I did, my mother always had a better plan for me. Eventually, I simply patronized her. I let her talk. Her old words -- I'd heard them a hundred times -- couldn't compete with my new life and its marvelous immediacy.

"You know," she'd say, "Your friends won't tell you the truth; only a mother can tell you that. If I only listened to my mother," she'd add, and then, "She was always right."

I know my choices came from the circumstances of my life, circumstances that she had not planned on -- for starters, the poverty that came with the Depression and then World War II. The Depression and the war invaded our kitchen. Though World War II did not take place in our country, and color television hadn't been invented to bring it into our living rooms, the bombs' echoes reached our ears, and their smoke colored our lives. When I think of the war, I think gray. The war remains a gray winter lasting four years.

Returning soldiers told us their foxhole dreams: steak smothered in onions, sweethearts, and a cozy home. During air-raid drills, sitting on the floor in the school corridor, singing songs that longed for "bluebirds over the white cliffs of Dover," I wanted those things too.

By then I was twelve years old; my mother's accident, the poverty during the depression, and the war's crusade for the simple life were dramatic on-going lessons from which I drew my own conclusions. My mother couldn't talk them away.

In her efforts to protect our childhood, she had mocked materialist values, "Who needs that!" she'd say if I described jewelry or a luxury a friend might have. She showed me a column by Leonard Lyons describing a society event and the hit some beautiful young women made "wearing only their youth": "And you see . . . 'only their youth.'" Another time, when a neighbor complimented her tan (she'd just hung the wash), she said, "I told him, 'The sun shines on poor people too.'" She'd argue, ask, how much did we need? Then sing, "I've got the sun in the morning and the moon at night," from the show *Annie Get Your Gun*.

But once she thought I could afford "things," she was annoyed with me for *not* accumulating them. I understood that she had wanted to spare us the hunger for what we couldn't afford, but continued to find happiness the old way. Life forced compromises, and she was shocked at the ones I chose to make: "You're like from the Middle Ages," she'd say.

*   *   *

All along, I'd been advised that women could do anything and needed a profession, but as a child when I came home from school to an empty unkempt apartment, I'd think of my mother describing how she would run the house if she didn't have to work for food on the table. That intention, as good as the act itself would have been, comforted me. I had wanted to come home to the homes my friends returned to after school. I would have like to be greeted by an orderly house and a smiling mother.

Once the war ended, and the post-war economy was robust, my mother found new challenges. She began to travel. She was among the first to go to Russia in the early sixties. At eighty she went to Israel alone, and there, against everyone's advice, took a bus to Egypt by herself -- not even on a tour. Among my mother's many accomplishments, she became a licensed beautician. Earlier, she had bought herself a car (with a stick shift) and then learned to drive. At 65, she learned to ride a bicycle; still later, she learned to swim, to crochet. She wasn't going to miss a thing. I was happy for her.

Now, standing in the kitchen, the memories rush through me like the last minutes in a busy dream. We leave the beets, prepared for a soup I will not taste, and go to a diner on Queens Boulevard for lunch.

My mother sips the hot tea -- a comfort in the overly air-conditioned dining room. Before I realize what's happening, the diner's lights brighten. Sheets of rain roll off the roof. Raindrops, like glass spikes racing down a windy pass, pitch toward the window, only to roll slowly, innocently, down. Outside, a woman takes off her shoes and runs barefoot on the sidewalk; a young couple laughs, holding newspapers over their heads. An older man stands in a doorway, lights a cigarette, and patiently yields to the deluge.

I sit and watch my mother as she enjoys the rain. I think back to times when she saved her good shoes from a downpour. We smile at each other, remembering how we laughed, running together in an unexpected shower. The rain's intensity slows to a misty drizzle.

She holds a packet of sugar in her left hand, stabbing the forefinger of her right hand against the paper, tearing it. Grains of sugar leak onto the table, but she does not notice, and so does not clean it up as she would have in better days, quickly and with a firm hand.

I watch her toy with the packet, knowing that she would like a cube of sugar, which she would place, Russian style, between her teeth, as she drinks her tea. But I cannot give her that sweetness.

Sitting there, in the quiet, I know it will be impossible to care for her as I had hoped, when I had wished her a long life. Now, I'm the one who is disappointed in how things are working out.

V

Leaving Elmhurst

Somehow, I always felt I had to take care of her --
protect her. One story was told so often I can picture it
happening. We are on a crowded bus; I am a tiny two-year-
old. A kind man hears me complain that I am tired. He
gives me his seat. I immediately turn to the passenger
seated next to me, and in a voice which, I was told, was
deep and low even then -- a surprise with my delicate blond
complexion -- demand, "You, give my mother a seat!"

But these days, my mother, already in her late
eighties, does not accept my demanding a seat for her. As
her strength weakens, she does not delegate any authority
to me, so intent is she on maintaining her position. I, her
daughter, am forbidden to take charge. My sister, six years
older, is not available; divorced, living in California,

struggling with a graphic arts business, she has distanced herself from the family.

Both my mother and I know that now she is not able to go back to past regrets and settle scores -- like the visit that had brought us to Becky Lieb almost a year ago. Now she needs all her energy to simply hold on to the present.

Knowing this much, she contacted a social worker at Elmhurst Hospital to help her (the hospital is about five blocks from her home). She tells me that she and this woman are friends. I do not know whether this friendship developed after she had been rushed there with heart failure a few times, after calling 911, or if they knew each other from my mother's volunteer work a few years earlier.

After my brother Simon died, my mother, who was past 80, worked as a translator and ombudsman for the Russian immigrants who were moving into the neighborhood. Her work began with Sara, whom she had met in a bakery, and to whom she was teaching English. Sara could not make herself understood to the doctor, so my mother translated for her and steered her through the hospital bureaucracy. The hospital suggested my mother volunteer to help other Russian patients. She had to get away from Simon's ghost, though she often said she would have been happy to trade places with him in the grave.

At the hospital, she wore a peach colored smock and a nameplate that identified her as a volunteer. She was given a free lunch. More important, Russian words that she never realized she knew flowed from her mouth, and the doctors, needing those words, spoke through her. But she stopped doing this work because the clinic never gave her enough time to schedule her visits. She would receive an urgent call as soon as a patient arrived. Then my mother would have to drop what she was doing and rush over to the hospital -- clear proof, she argued, that no one respected her time.

However, she had learned about services provided and how to get them. It was her understanding that she was entitled to an aide a few mornings a week. She was adamant that I was never to show my face at the hospital. "You are too much of a child; you would not know how to handle it," she said. I was over fifty then. So the only time I did go there was to sign her out and bring her to my home.

Now she tells me that a man and woman have come to her house to investigate. I am concerned, and torn between respecting her independence and protecting her. My impression is that these strangers, friends I never met, are replacing me. I wonder if they can be trusted to understand her needs. Are they really who they say they are?

I finally learn that the hospital referred her to the Jewish Associated Services for the Aged, JASA. Debbie Weinberg, a young social worker there, is genuinely sympathetic and warm to my mother. She talks to her and helps her with practical matters. She helps her avoid a rent increase. My mother calls her often. The week I go on a vacation, Debbie checks in with her daily.

I speak to Debbie also, and she is as kind to me. She tells me all is going well, and helps me fill out forms. She says, "Not to worry."

My mother's doctors tell me that now she has temporary ischemia and intermittent claudication, not uncommon in a woman of her age. That means her blood flow is not reliable and that for a few minutes she is totally drained; those moments are lost. Then, as soon as the blood starts going again, she is my mother again, as the doctor says, "chairman of the board." It is hard to buck the chairman of the board. She is in charge, in demeanor, but has to harness her efforts for small decisions like food and clothing, and often these decisions are inappropriate.

So, although I do not understand the progress of senility and dementia, as time goes on I see that my mother is deteriorating. She refuses to cut her hair. Some time ago, she said she was letting it grow so that she could wear it in a bun, but she simply lets it hang loose. She points to young women, or teenage girls, and says, "It's the style," and what would I know, living in New Jersey. Nevertheless, she is beginning to look unkempt, wild. She is slowly shrinking; her clothes are too big for her and they are shabby. She never owned a cotton housedress, not even to change into. No, she'd wear long denim skirts with a shocking pink top, or update an old blouse by changing the collar, or add a fashionable chiffon scarf. Now, in a stained skirt, and loose blouse (the bold geometric pattern an insult to her fragility), she can no longer be taken for a chic lady at a Lincoln Center concert.

She had always been so pretty. My son, Zach told me how, at Simon's funeral five years ago, friends and colleagues who had taught English with him had commented on how pretty she was, and at such a terrible time. But now, vague, frail, her white hair long and wispy, propelled along a busy street of purposeful shoppers and diligent store owners, she looks like a costumed character out of a children's fairy tale.

It is summer again. Debbie has worked it out so that an aide will help her twice a week. I am hopeful, that they will make things easier. These aides are "disabled" women who are being "job-trained." When my mother complains about the aide, I am not surprised. But to check her out, I stop by, before one of our outings, and introduce myself.

The aide, a heavy white woman, who appears to be polite though distant, barely answers my greeting. I figure she is tired and hot (later I will think, sullen). We leave when she says her work is done.

Then we are off to Rockaway Beach, a great pleasure for my mother. Usually, when I drive her back home, I leave her in front of her building, but this time I go up to the apartment. The aide has cleaned the stove and left the gas on. Because of the air-conditioning, all the windows are closed and the apartment is essentially sealed.

The next day, I ask for a new aide; that one forgets

to replug the refrigerator. The following morning, my mother has to mop up over an inch of water. Then, when I call to complain, the woman in charge comes to the aide's defense; she offers no sympathy and says, "Just because she forgot to put the plug in, I'm not going to fire her." So much for entitlements.

Debbie recommends a private agency, and I pay for it without letting my mother know. The new aide, Beverly, is efficient, gentle and non-judgmental because she has worked with others who were going through my mother's present situation, and so better understands what is happening. Beverly comes every morning. She makes sure my mother takes her pills, which are in a shoe box on the end table next to her bed. I sort her pills into individual envelopes, with the date and dosage labeled in bright blue magic marker. At my mother's suggestion, the envelope contains still another, smaller, envelope, labeled in bright orange, which contains the evening pill.

By now, I am calling Debbie probably as often as my mother does, and she is always reassuring. Often I combine a visit to my mother with a visit to her. I tell Debbie about the day my mother called me and laughed because she couldn't find her way home from A&S, the department store. It's just a few blocks from her house, and she'd been going there regularly for coffee and company. Debbie assures me the policemen in Queens spend half their time escorting old ladies back to their homes. When I tell Debbie how much more paranoid my mother has become -- describing men looking into her windows, her constant fear that she will be put out of the building -- Debbie suggests bringing a psychiatrist to my mother's apartment.

I am there for that interview. Her apartment is clean and inviting. She has even placed a few cookies on a dish in the center of the table in the kitchen. Her hair is neatly coifed, and her demeanor thoughtful. Somehow, maybe because Debbie is present, there is no tension. We sit comfortably in the studio's living room. The psychiatrist, a balding man in his late fifties, questions my mother about the people she says are looking in her window. She admits it isn't clear, almost hinting that it could be part of a dream. When he asks how she feels in regard to her health, she admits that she tires easily, and answers other questions on how she manages, and what other problems she may have, thoughtfully and logically. I am impressed that he is not patronizing. He prescribes 25 mg of melaril, a very low dosage of a mood-altering drug, and assures me that my mother is in much better shape than many other old people living alone. I think of our lunch that rainy day in the diner, and begin to look for nursing homes.

I had checked a few when my mother had been so unhappy at Sunnyside Lodge the previous year, recovering from her bout of gastro-enteritis. A cousin of hers had stayed at the Riverdale Home for the Aged. There, the residents sold their arts and craft works; the money went for trips -- once to Israel. Although it was highly regarded, we thought it much too large. My mother then agreed to look at The Hebrew Home for the Aged in New Rochelle, where my husband's aunt had resided. Shifra was a very particular woman, whose children were caring and concerned. So my mother thought it might be acceptable.

That visit was such a fiasco that I stopped looking. As soon as we entered the home, the social worker insisted on interviewing us. My mother immediately let her know that we were only looking. The social worker persisted and demanded her address, her doctor's name, hospitalizations, and other particulars. My mother could not bear it and grabbed the form and tore it up. That day, my mother and I left Sunnyside Lodge and met a friend who knew my mother well. She shook her head, as if to say, "This won't do!" But I knew that my mother was afraid of being investigated.

She had received a blood transfusion several years before, when she had been operated on for stomach cancer. Then, about a month before that day in New Rochelle, in the course of a routine physical in Queens, her doctor requested a urine sample. On that night, the evening news announced that it was discovered that many people who had blood transfusions at the time my mother did had contracted AIDS. The transfusion and the coincidence of the day's urine sample and the evening news convinced her that not only was she at risk, but that she was suspect, despite repeated assurances by her doctor that this was not so. But, she reasoned, why else would the people in her building ask her to sign forms about tenants' rights. Whatever sense it made to her, it was not information she cared to share with an officious social worker. Needless to say, she failed the interview. The social worker said, "At this time, your mother is not a candidate for our institution. Maybe she would be better with home care." Maybe.

Although she has managed for almost a year since that interview, I know she cannot continue living on her own. Her tenuous hold on reality makes me nervous about her safety in the apartment. I am determined to find a nursing home, and so look at several that Debbie Weinberg recommends in New York, and also at a few in New Jersey. Each time, as soon as I enter the lobby, I have to submit to "the interview." Usually I'm kept waiting while the social workers are on the phone to a husband or baby sitter, or, once, checking whether a personal package had been delivered. I am seldom asked if I have any questions, nor am I permitted to look at the facility, but I have to answer their questions regarding my mother's money, her age, her health, and her competence. I understand my mother's unrestrained impulse the previous year, and ache to grab the printed forms. A crazy nerve has been stroked, her full name on the paper, Anna Kreminetsky Trefman, outlines her life. I think of her first port of entry -- her name there: suddenly the forms are as crucial as passports.

Despite their lilting voices, their manicured nails, their vacuous smiles, their fashionable outfits, the social workers remind me of stories I'd heard about the immigration guards at Ellis Island, whose contempt for immigrants resulted in misspelled names which desecrated family lines. Even worse, they had the power to deny entry.

The first time my mother's father tried to enter America, he had been sent back to Russia because of a heart condition. The second time he came with his family, but died on the way. He was buried in Italy. My mother, the oldest, had carried her Gymnasium diploma and a letter of acceptance to the Brooklyn School of Pharmacy, then had to work in a shirt factory to support her mother and four younger children. She had had such high hopes. In Russia, she was one of only two in her village to go to Gymnasium (the Russian high school), one that boasts distinguished authors among its alumni. This revealed as much about opportunities there as it did about her brightness and fortitude; her father had arranged for a milkman to drive her in his wagon in the mornings; she'd walk the five miles back each day.

Now she would be entering her last port. I look upside down at the forms and wonder what the information on them will determine. I wish I had the courage to tear up the forms as my mother had -- and destroy our need for the facility as well. Instead I whisper my thanks for their time and escape from the buildings. I have seen enough anyway: a glimpse of old men and women tied to wheelchairs.

I remember when she was well and strong -- we may have been visiting someone; at the time it wasn't our problem -- she said, "When choosing a place, don't make it a situation that is easy for *you*. If ever I need to go to a home, remember, I'll be the one to be there; each minute there will be mine."

Then it was all merely conjecture. I don't know what I had imagined. Did I expect my mother to be on the Riviera, watering bougainvilleas surrounding a sundrenched chateau, her sweetheart standing in the shadows nearby? Closer to home, now I only wish she could read her books, choose her clothes, sew a button on her skirt, or rinse her blouse in her own bathroom sink. When I was a child I would watch her wash her stockings after long walks in the city. She'd look at the dirty water and say, "See, my stockings thank me."

But now that these simple tasks are so difficult, I know that what she needs is a place that provides services. What complicates the search is that I'd learned that each home has three levels of care, and the quality of each level is not uniform in each facility. In a Workmen's Circle Home, the top level, Health Related care, where the residents are usually mobile and lucid, its programs and activities are so appealing that, in my exhausted state, I could consider a short stay for myself. But I do not feel that way about their Intermediate Care.

Intermediate Care has the broadest range of quality among the homes I visit. The residents, who might manage some of their personal needs, like feeding and washing themselves, are often in wheelchairs, physically weaker than those in Health Related. Some are in the early stages of Alzheimer's. In most homes, seated in dark halls, they are encouraged not to walk (although one had an accordion player entertain, and another had sing-alongs).

In the Skilled Nursing level the patients are totally dependent, and I have to find a way to gauge compassion and care.

I focus on Intermediate Care, where I know my mother belongs, even though the visiting nurse had decided on Health Related: my mother revs herself up for guests, and appears less mixed-up during formal visits (there is no talk about faces in the window), but I am afraid that she will continue to deteriorate.

No home in New York accepts a resident without a visiting nurse credential, a PRI. Debbie helps me organize this. I must coordinate a time that the visiting nurse and I can agree on and have the forms completed for them. Also, as I look at nursing homes, I have to respect the standards my mother worked for all her life. I do not understand all the ramifications of her condition only that it is progressive, and racing like a current I cannot halt.

I have not yet found a nursing home, but I am learning what to look for, as I am confronted with the overwhelming despair, the smells, the cost. I want time and I want speed. It is all taking so long and happening so quickly.

Suddenly, on Sunday morning, Labor Day weekend (exactly a year since our ill-fated visit to Becky), Beverly, her health aide calls to tell me she will not stay with my mother today. She's gotten a job with more hours. She promises to come in the mornings and take care of my mother's meds. Maybe she will return at another time.

It will be impossible to get another aide. The tennis matches are on in nearby Forest Hills, so my husband Ralph and daughter Laura decide to drive me in, watch a few sets, while I visit and check on my mother. But when I get there, I cannot find her.

As I have done many times before, I case her haunts: the benches in front of the library, a coffee shop nearby, the A&S shopping mall. She is not in any of those places. The streets are empty. One neighbor, Dennis, the building's unofficial doorman, tells me that he's seen her earlier, walking.

I let myself into her apartment, go to the bathroom, wash. I comb my hair in the dressing alcove and notice that the high summer sun has found a path into her room, which suddenly feels bright and dear. I see its order: the low chair near the television, the nubby gold couch, on one side, a dresser with books and a radio on it, a white marble coffee table, the small yellow tub chairs that define the living room area, and, next to the wall, her bed covered with a Mexican blanket. The room a wash of oranges and

gold, lovely white lamps, and scattered pillows, crocheted
in purple and blue -- the one sure clue that an old woman
lives there.

I look across to the kitchen, to the large table where
she has taught so many casual acquaintances English and
where she has rolled the dough for her famous apple pies. I
see how cleverly she has composed her space -- and how she
cherishes it. I miss her presence. My dread keeps building
even as I look at the sun, which I have never seen there
before. I am unsure of what I have to do or whether I will
be able to do it.

After a short time, Ralph and Laura come back.
They are uneasy about my mother's situation, her
disorientation, and the fact that she is suddenly without
the aide's limited care. Just moments after they enter the
apartment, a neighbor, who lives in the apartment above,
brings my mother in, mixed-up: she went to his apartment
instead. She follows him docilely, and makes no excuses;
she says nothing -- a clear, sad picture which tells us how
she is.

After thanking the neighbor, and hugging my
mother, Ralph says, actually orders, "We must bring her
back; she can't stay here alone any more. I'll get the car
and wait." He leaves. Laura and I hardly speak. We just
start packing. My sister Bernice, totally unaware of my
mother's condition, calls from California. I am glad that
she has called, since my mother misses her terribly.
Bernice tells her how bad business is and how worried she

is. I try to tell Bernice what is going on, but she cannot listen.

My mother, now worried about my sister, doesn't want to go to my house. She wants to help Bernice. However, I cannot afford to take on another project, and stick to the matter at hand: "We're going now, Mom," I say. I do not make the usual promises about returning after a few days.

She insists I bring the last painting left on her wall, a large picture of a country road in the rural South that has always reminded her of her childhood home in Bessarabia, a region in southwestern Russia. It is heavy and cumbersome; I take it along with the suitcases.

A Different Mother

VI

The Picture over the Couch

Laura takes my mother by the hand, "Would you like a cup of tea Nannawanni? ("Nannawanni," Laura's baby talk for Grandma Anna, became the name all the children used.) My mother ignores her, and follows me, as I carry the painting into David's room. Because I am afraid its glass might break, I hang it up immediately. The glass, which had protected the picture for so many years, eerily reflects my mother's face as it was when she had affectionately examined its scene so long ago.

"That's what it was like, a dirt road. That was the same, the *blutta*," she says (I'd forgotten the Yiddish word for mud, which suddenly comes out of the picture). So many stories about her childhood had included a reference to the melting mud roads -- the *blutta*. "But no telephone poles," she says on further scrutiny, "We had only kerosene lamps."

Back then, even with the picture on our living room wall, when she told her stories I had never visualized that treeless plain. I had imagined many houses close together, a forest: a combination of the Lower East Side and colonial America.

The picture was brought to our new apartment in the west Bronx by an artist friend, an old friend of my parents. I was nine years old and felt buoyed by its magical power: a person had come out of the past. Also, our family had arrived, spending both time and money on "ART." I only listened, reveling in the luxury of the talk, thinking that surely this picture was a sign of the good times in store for us. Its size alone lifted my spirits. Finally, I thought, we were like other families; we too, had a large picture over the living room couch.

My mother hadn't chosen the picture merely to fill a space. Although it was an original colored lithograph, signed by the artist, the link to her childhood was what she treasured most.

Oddly enough, though it had always reminded my mother of her home in Bessarabia, now, when I look at it, it evokes my childhood home in the west Bronx. My memory of events there are clear. There is no confusion, I can feel myself in those rooms and hear her voice as if I were there. The picture -- which I had brought at the insistence of a weak, sick old woman -- hanging on the wall in my son's room, brings back the vibrant life she created for us.

Our new apartment house had an open courtyard,

with three levels leading to two separate entrances which we thought was quite fancy. Walking through it, we'd pass grown-ups sitting on folding chairs, boys playing stickball, or girls jumping rope. At times, we had to maneuver around a swift game of "slug," where you hit the ball with your hand -- one bounce to the wall. None of this interfered with our feeling of elegance. There was also greenery, a bit of unpaved earth that held a spring rain, whose earthy smell was faintly felt through every day's bus exhaust. The lone tree in the center of the courtyard's top level, protected by a low spiked fence, and the short privet bushes surrounding the rest of the building were meant to mark the seasons and prove that we did not live in a tenement, even though we had five flights to climb.

Just as new as this special entrance were our neighbors, richer Americans, who, except for an old lady with a dog, spoke English without a foreign accent. Chester, the bulldog, named after Chester Laabs, a 1940 baseball player, only understood commands in Yiddish, and wouldn't learn English no matter how much the neighborhood boys tormented him. He would look at the woman with his enormous bulging eyes, she'd whisper something to him in Yiddish, and then he'd roll over -- content.

On warm days through open windows one could hear children practicing the piano, families fighting -- each member standing up for himself. The sense of place is clear, its exuberance unmistakable. I would learn how differently each family saw the good life.

We were not quite as assimilated into American life or as conventional as our new neighbors. We still spoke Yiddish, our family code, for jokes, rages, and songs. The language itself protected the past. I was quite aware of our differences, but I felt no deprivations. I enjoyed my family, especially in our new prosperity; visitors did as well. Whatever we did, without introductions or excuse, as I am now reminded, the passion poured out; though our furnishings did not quite measure up to theirs, they would often comment on the new bookcases that suddenly appeared. Music too!

Simon (the quietest one), back from stick-ball on the streets, would be conducting symphonies by different composers, or listening to the hillbilly folk-songs of his record collection.

Bernice would be deep in concentration, perfecting a passage from Bach's Fifteen Two-part Inventions on the black upright piano. Otherwise, she'd be designing sets or costumes for theatre productions (at college and at the Traphagen School of Design). She always seemed apart from the rest of us, working hard to join the world beyond.

My mother, busy cooking, would review American movies in such a way that we easily imagined, possibly expected, Spencer Tracy to sit and talk with us. My father would be buried in a book or newspaper. In the commotion, a raucous joke might erupt, but no fights, fights were private. As voices rose, windows slammed, "the neighbors shouldn't hear!"

My friends, and my sister's and brother's friends, took it all in, and often said, "This is a perfect family for a book," or, "You're like, the movie *You Can't Take It With You*." But to me, families in movies, fairytales, or books like *The Bobbsey Twins* had no relevance to my life. Books or movies weren't supposed to be about people like us.

Nevertheless, as good as times promised to be, I noticed other differences between our family and our new neighbors. Little things at first, like the pot of hot coffee on their stoves, and how it emptied as the day progressed. Our Pyrex coffeepot was seldom used. My parents preferred tea -- and drank it from a glass, holding a cube of sugar between their teeth, an economy she learned in Russia during the revolution. My mother didn't need coffee for energy (as I do). She was always moving: cooking, shopping, cleaning, sewing, all performed with deftness and intensity. She'd often sing or recite a poem as she worked. The idea of a singing commercial could have started in our house. Why, even when she applied makeup to run down the five flights to shop for food, she'd sing. Sitting on the bathtub rim, I'd watch her. She'd catch my eye in the medicine cabinet's mirror, and sing in Yiddish,

> A little powder
> A little rouge
> Two pillows on the side (here she'd tap her full breasts)
> And so we get a husband.

65

Then, down for fresh milk and bread, vegetables, and her usual battle with the butcher. On her return, we'd hear the adventure: the new potatoes were out, so delicate, or corn (how her mother had loved corn!), or the greens might be especially fresh. "Just wait and see how good dinner will be," she'd promise, bursting with a story to tell . . . or retell. The butcher encounter was her classic.

"'No, I don't want that one,' I told him, 'I want the one in front,'" she'd say, when he'd take the meat from the case, mimicking the tone she used in the butcher-shop, a tone so urgent, I felt myself jostled by customers.

"I told him, 'Give me what I ask for! I can still choose.' I told him, 'I can still choose.' I'm not that old," and then she'd smile at me. I had to hear the story a few times, before I understood that my "old" mother, not yet forty, meant she was not too old to choose a man. For me, her perpetual glow was independent of romance. I had no idea what men and women did, nor could I imagine why my mother, already married, would want to choose . . . a man. My father, twenty years older, skulking around our lives, was so remote he was not even a shadow. At any rate, I was certain her "choosing" was limited to her open flirtations in shops and streets, and was simply an expression of her zest for life.

I think of my mother's voice during those times. Though she spoke English fluently, she never lost her accent: "w's" remained "v's," and the emphasis was usually on the last syllable. Her voice was not particularly low, nor was it pitched high, but she played with it when telling a story. Often, one sentence could be loud and soft, hold anger and joy, and float from English to Yiddish and, with a nod to my father, to Russian; her words like her life, tumbled. She never hesitated. Now she does -- now that she is old.

I realize that I do not know exactly how old she is. There's a five-year range, 1901 or 1905. "I'm old enough," she would say. The date was equally vague, "sometime in the summer;" the family settled on July 12. (Her sister's birthday was Purim -- never mind that, on the lunar calendar, Purim could fall a month apart from one year to the next.) So I settle on 1901, which makes her 88 years old. Why should her slowness shock me so?

She had not expected to be poor. Marrying in the 1920's she had had a taste of luxury: She loved the feel of soft wool, fine silk, dresses made with French seams -- her pleasure in them all was sensual, not pretentious. She scorned amateur opera in the same way. For her, the essence of opera was its grandeur; the sets, costumes and voices had to measure up to the emotional extremes in opera's intrigues and music.

My mother would rhapsodize about the pause in *Madame Butterfly*, "When she waits for her lover . . . the waiting . . . Rena . . . ." And she'd sit on the couch with a Mona Lisa smile, her eyes lowered, her palm up in a stop pose, not allowing me to interrupt the silence. "The waiting . . . ," and she'd nod as if she had done such waiting herself.

I loved her comments on opera or literature, but whenever she referred to luxury, I thought it was an abstraction.

All the singing and talk could not hide how hard she worked. After the war she moved on to sewing coats and suits. On hot summer days she would come home from work and I would lay cold compresses on her upper arms, red from rubbing against her sides as she pushed woolen coats through the machine for the coming winter. Because she was paid by the piece, by the amount produced, haggling over pennies for each seam was expected whenever a new style was introduced. She'd bring those battles to our crowded kitchen, relishing the play by play.

On one of those summer evenings, she laughed as she told me about a woman who complained about the garment factory job my mother had found for her. The woman had told my mother, "When I come home I'm so tired I think I'm dead."

"I told her," my mother continued as if she were lying on the beach, "that's only in the beginning; later when you hold the money in your hand, you'll feel alive.'"

For her, life was a celebration, clothing as important as necessities; styles took care of the seasons -- blossoming flowers made no show on our cement streets. "Who needs it? This is also spring," she'd say, admiring us all in our finery. Our coats and suits were made during the "slow season," when workers pooled their labor and sewed outfits for each other's families (the manufacturer sold them the fabric wholesale). My mother worked for quality "houses," and during my teens I always wore good suits and coats -- my mother, so close to the fashion world, was happy she could dress me in style.

If I hinted that she worked too hard, if there was any sympathy in my voice, she'd tell me how when her arm was broken and a woman had been sent to the house to wash her kitchen floor, she had envied her. No, working hard was good. Incredulously, she'd tell me about the rich, who joined expensive clubs to play hard enough to sweat. "Don't complain about hard work. They're paying me for it." Yes, working hard was good; the six a.m. subway rush-hour trip was dismissed: "Everyone smells of toothpaste -- anywhere else but here, people would be groped or knifed. Don't complain." Life was grand. And we had our own mountains, skyscrapers -- a tribute to man, not God. "Whoever passes 42nd Street," she'd say of her beloved city, "only one time they'd have to be here, and they will have a tombstone here."

Maybe it was the fashion center that kept her so committed to improving everyone's looks. She'd even spruce up the cacti, placing rubber bands on them "to make them more attractive." We'd say she was "giving them a Toni," the home permanents that were popular then. Once, Bernice gave my mother the permanent and I did the haircut (I'd given many haircuts to the counselors in summer camp). My mother marched into our neighbor's apartment to show off.

"So, how do you like my Rena's haircut? Look what she did to me" (I had cut curled bangs, a totally new look). In that dim foyer, her unguarded pleasure reminded me that she'd been a girl -- before the plumpness, when the black in her hair had been her own. I imagined her teasing Russian boyfriends, or flirting with my father in his bookstore, where they met.

Our neighbor next door and her two children had emigrated from Austria "just in time," though her husband had not been that fortunate. She worked in a dress factory, and the two women often talked together in her kitchen. One evening, I wanted to tell my mother something -- a joke I'd heard on the radio, or a problem about preparing dinner the next day; whatever it was, I often joined them. When I rang the bell and opened the door, my mother's welcome surprised me, "Here comes my darling little one," she almost sang. Why? What had I done? I looked around to check if it was really me who had made her glow. With her, a compliment came out of nowhere, like a sudden splash of water, or a cat on the fire escape.

For her, ironing was joyful -- to make a crumpled rag come alive. She and Bernice made ironing an art form. I remember pink and white starched blouses and skirts

70

cooling in our foyer; that Saturday smell of the hot iron and starch heralded spring as definitely as any freshly cut lawn or blooming azaleas do for me now in suburbia. My mother would stand next to baskets of ironing, shouting to the cadence of Alfred Noyes' poem, "The Highwayman": "I'll get it done by moonlight, I'll finish it by moonlight, I'll finish it by moonlight," and here she'd pause, take a deep breath, and say the bad word, "though Hell should bar my way!"

I take another look at the picture that I had thought would change our lives: her home -- a few cabins on a muddy lane under a raging sunset. A young girl, who will walk in man-made canyons and welcome the sweet spring in the new styles of coats and suits, lived there.

In all the tumult, I had gotten one message right after all. At the very end, when she was as weak and as vague as she would become, the staff at a wonderful nursing home would tell me about her requests for "bread and butter for the children," my brother, sister, and me. She was still a mother. On her night wanderings, the staff would give her bread and tea. She would forage some, "for the children." They told me this to assure me that she was connected to us.

And I did feel reassured. "If I only could," she had said, "I would bake pies every day for you."

A Different Mother

VII

Applying for Sunnyside Lodge

But now she is at my home. Everything looks too big
on her. Wearing her blue checked blouse and a black skirt,
she holds on to -- no, pushes against -- the deck railing, a
prisoner, despite the picnic paraphernalia: the grill, the
open bag of charcoal, the yellow lounge chairs, all
suggesting an easy freedom from the confines of winter.
Her eyes squint as if they are facing a bright sun, but the
sky is gray. They narrow from a particular exquisite pain
that I cannot assuage. "Take me back to my house," she
weeps. The trees sway, heavy with leaves gilded a blazing
orange: autumn is coming. The air is humid and thick
with pollen. Soon her hands hold her face, and she is
kneeling, imploring, "They will take it away!" She pulls at
her hair, grasps her neck. And this is not the first time.

"Mom, I promise you, they will not take your
apartment. I will call the landlord on Tuesday. The office
is closed now. You can talk to them."

The kitchen door is open. I am talking as I stand at the sink, wringing a dishrag, twisting tightly -- no water left. How many times have I made that promise this Labor Day weekend? I have also dialed so that she can see that the office isn't open. Tired and helpless, I go to her, try again to embrace her, but am pushed away, and wonder how we came to this moment.

When we brought her to my house yesterday, I was worried about her condition. But I had no idea how much she has changed and how different it will be from the other times she stayed with us not more than a month ago. She cries most of the time, begging to go back to her apartment, and worries that they will take it away. She stands on the deck screaming -- no words -- silent tantrums that will continue to haunt my daughter.

I try reasoning in an even voice, but soon hear myself screaming through her screams: "Your apartment will not, cannot be taken from you!" I promise her again and again that on Tuesday I will call the landlord, but does she understand when Tuesday will come? We are both in new territory.

I look back and think of the enormous amount of work and jokes and arguments and songs and dresses and lessons and then think how surprised I am that she got old.

I am not sure whether I cannot see what is happening, or if I cannot face what is happening. Her behavior is so erratic. I hope that rest and care will bring her back to herself. I take her to our doctor, who is now her doctor as well. He readjusts her medications. She improves, is more rational, less agitated, but it is clear she can no longer live alone. After all, she couldn't even find her own apartment. And we cannot depend on aides -- good or bad, they just don't last.

My mother, resigned, says she wants to go back to Sunnyside Lodge, the nursing home near my house. I also like the idea that the Lodge is close, but I have reservations about it. Sunnyside Lodge calls itself a retirement home and caters mostly to wealthy women from established families, families with property that included horses and fences, women who never worked, women who played bridge, shopped a lot, and in some cases enjoyed tracing their ancestry to revolutionary times. I worry that, over the long haul, my immigrant mother will not fit in. Not that she isn't sophisticated or cultured, in fact, in her own way she is probably more so than they.

Although my mother has worked in a factory, she read Pasternak in Russian, and, when reading Hemingway, read deeper than the plot. Often she would talk about *The Old Man and the Sea*: "And you see . . . ," she would say, "he has to be cunning to catch the fish. He is not young and strong anymore." She loved opera enough to go standing room only -- during the "slow season" when she worked in the New York garment district. Paying for her pleasures by hard work or hard cash increased them. If she were well, she would not choose to be with these women.

75

I talked about these differences with my older son, Zach, when my mother stayed at the Lodge the first time. Zach and she are very good friends. He loves her dearly, laughs with her, brought his friends to be entertained by her in her little apartment. At that time he assured me that the ladies at the Lodge would find her "pleasantly exotic." Possibly they did. She didn't exactly make friends then, but the young owners and the landscapers had found her entertaining.

This time she is not the same, and it isn't as if I have many choices or much time. I feel I can't discuss this decision with my sister. She is far away with problems of her own. Besides, I know that she could not imagine my mother helpless and unable to run her own show. As for my husband, Ralph, should I ask, he would help in any way possible. He does help, by not questioning or interrupting my rhythm; pretty much the way I had been when he placed his parents in a nursing home some ten years ago. Without talking, we know that having to do this is as private as it is difficult. I understand that the Lodge is not the perfect solution, but it will have to do for now.

I think back to the day when Baruch's daughter, Shoshana, visited the Lodge, about a year ago, during that first stay. We'd had lunch on the deck at my house. In the evening, when we brought my mother back to the Lodge, Shoshana came with us. She said, "Compared to the nursing homes in Israel, this is The Garden of Eden."

This time, my mother, aware that she is "declining," as she describes her situation, says she is willing to make concessions. On a visit to the doctor, he reminds her that on her previous stay she wandered off the grounds. "Now, I won't run away," she promises. Turning aside, she looks out his office window, where she intently watches as a small red car backs out onto the road and speeds away. The doctor tells me he'll recommend her; I chew on my lips, hoping we'll be lucky.

Because she'd been so critical of the place the last time, unwilling to stay, "to sit like a *groomed dog*" among the women, as she said, and because of my own doubts about it, I suggest we look at another home as well. She greets this idea thoughtfully; her face becomes still, which makes me wonder if she is looking back at her stronger self, or ahead to the interview, or even worse, to her incarceration, as she considers what to do to make a good impression.

"First, I must get my hair cut," she says. Then she chooses her outfit, a neat white shirt, a blue broadcloth skirt, and my daughter's tailored beige linen jacket to complete it. With her new hair cut, rest, and a sense of purpose, she looks elegant. We practice for the interview by reviewing the questions we expect them to ask: her age, the date and who is president. College interviews cannot be more harrowing.

She is so convincing that the social worker at The Daughters of Miriam suggests an apartment that includes strong support services: housekeeping, meals in a dining room, medical supervision. Seated behind my mother, I vigorously shake my head against it. I know he sees me. For a second I catch his sneaky eye. Sucking in his bottom lip he goes on. Soon I'll know why.

Finally, my mother tires and tells him he cannot recognize her trouble. "I fooled you, but never mind; it is a good place."

The social worker responds by reminding us that she isn't a New Jersey resident. "You might be lucky; a place in Health Related might open up," he says, adding, "if you pay a non-refundable $40,000 in advance."

My mother ambles out of the office, and I am not ashamed to ask, "Even if she dies the next day?" "In advance," is his succinct reply.

I am relieved that her first choice is Sunnyside Lodge. She is familiar with it; she repeats that she enjoyed the meals in the dining room. I set up an interview.

The woman who interviews my mother there remembers her from the year before and remarks on the change in her. "Oh, she's forgetting. She's forgetting," she sighs.

She assigns my mother to Intermediate Care, and explains that less will be expected of her now than before. She tells us my mother can be admitted a few days later, payment due one month in advance. The rate will be higher; $110 rather than $95 per day. While the money set aside for this purpose will not last indefinitely, at least she will be taken care of while I look for a nursing home that accepts Medicare.

My mother is satisfied. She has chosen the place and will be near me. I have stopped thinking. I am moving like a robot, with no sense of time or self to wonder how it will work out, as I need all my energy to manage each moment.

The next day I am busy -- washing, ironing, and mending her clothes. I am sewing name tags on them; it seems we have not spoken for a minute when I discover she is gone. I walk around the house, inside and out, calling to her. My neighbor's daughter-in-law joins me. We walk through the woods on soft decaying leaves, the fall beauty jarring, afraid she's fallen on a rock or tripped on the uneven terrain. For a moment, I actually wonder if that would be a more desirable end, a more equal foe -- more real than the mystery that is stealing her reason. We drive through the neighborhood, calling, but it is no use. I phone the police.

After looking for her in their car -- at least an hour and a half has passed -- the police are about to radio in for search dogs, when a new neighbor, who lives about a quarter of a mile down steep terrain, drives her back.

I ask the police not to report this, afraid that Sunnyside Lodge might find out and then not accept her.

The neighbor found her sitting in front of her house, which, though quite different from mine (green and white shingles to my natural cedar), is also contemporary: both have triangular windows. My mother scolds me for not being there. She asks if I'd made friends with the new neighbor, "a very nice woman."

When I had called Ralph at his office, and told him she was missing, he rushed home. Seeing she is safe, he welcomes her with a hug. "I wanted Sunnyside," she says to him, "and I got Sunnyside."

"Better than getting into Princeton, Momma," he says. I am happy that she has controlled her fate after all. But when I drive her there the next day and say, "So you got it," she is quick to answer, "So, what's so good about that?"

VIII

I Learn about Dementia

Sunnyside Lodge is a short drive from my home. I drive as slowly as possible, glancing at my mother. Our silence squashes the bravado about how lucky we are that she is going to Sunnyside. There are no words. Despite the Lodge's bright green lawn, the Indian summer day, I know my mother is deep in the winter of her life.

From the road, the lodge looks like an inviting motel in the Berkshires -- pale green siding, always freshly painted. Each room opens to the balcony, which wraps around the second floor. But we are not deceived.

Our family was friendly with the owners. The Edmond children now all work at the family business begun by John Edmond's mother. His wife had been a New Yorker -- from New Rochelle -- and since I came from the Bronx, we shared a vague commonality.

While I hadn't tricked my mother, I wonder if I have

tricked the Edmonds. My mother is not functioning well. I actually think she is out of place here. My cheeks prickle with embarrassment. I check myself -- the criteria have changed; she is old and sick -- she's been placed in Intermediate Care. Am I forgetting? Do I still see my mother as a person in working order?

The clearness of the day feels harsh, and the grass is too green, greener even than fall grass. I find its artificiality disquieting -- an omen. Inside, the social constraints the residents live by, so different from my mother's and mine seem disingenuous as well. They camouflage pain and despair; and with the collaboration of modern medicine, feign life as well as they can.

Sunnyside Lodge's interior is designed to look like a New England country inn. Its dining room has a red plaid rug and black wrought iron fixtures. The public rooms are large and airy, filled with leafy plants, blue carpeting, and polished maple colonial furniture. The facility has a small library with large print books. The spinet piano is closed. In fact, there is no music, though the silence holds a sound a dog could hear, a piercing high frequency whistle -- the sound of anguish repressed.

My mother is given a room on the second floor. I help her unpack, and hang her clothes in the closet she will share with her roommate, who seems to be a lovely woman -- soft spoken and polite. She welcomes us with a smile. Because of her rheumatism she can hardly move and sits by the window, reading. Like all other rooms, this one is large and clean. Consistently faithful to the colonial style throughout the building, it includes two beds, two bureaus, two bookcases, and two maple easy chairs with plaid cushions.

We place a family photograph, from David and Carol's wedding at our house that past June, on the bureau and go downstairs where several women sit watching television. My mother joins them.

"Is she confused?" a tall woman dressed in a brown tailored suit asks me, as she looks up from her newspaper, before saying hello to my mother.

"Sometimes," I answer. It isn't an absolute lie, but not quite the truth -- she can function, but clearly not as before and I am afraid that my mother will be rejected. The woman looks her over, looks at her clothes, even down at her shoes, and says, "It's a good place," and goes back to reading her newspaper, the *Star-Ledger*.

Then Bertha comes toward us; her broad smile brings back her 94th birthday celebration that we had attended the year before.

"Hey, I remember you," she says to my mother. "This place has changed since you were here."

"I can see that," my mother answers. She looks at the blue patterned wallpaper as though the walls had been painted a different color.

"Yeah, a lot more confused people," Bertha says.

"Is that so? I can see that," my mother says slowly. This time there is no conspiratorial comment on the shortcomings of others, and Bertha is savvy enough not to say any more. She notices everything, and I'm sure the change in my mother does not escape her. She simply raises her eyebrows and walks away.

From my mother's previous stay, I know that most of the residents are quiet and reserved. Then, a few had begged me for death: "I want to die," they had whispered to me as if I could give death to them.

I am not sure how much of that was part of the condition of their lives, and how much was due to the way the place is run. Yet now I am happy that my mother can stay here, vaguely aware that my limited choices have modified my standards. I comfort myself: it is so clean, so spacious, and close. I leave her waiting for dinner to be served, and I am hoping that, despite my reservations, she will be all right. I think I can make up for what is missing. In the car I try to release the tight smile I have cranked into my jaw.

The following morning, just as I am running the water for my coffee, the Lodge phones. A voice shouts my name, and then informs me that my mother has had a difficult night; she ransacked her roommate's drawers, emptied their shared closet, and spent the rest of the time, racing through the halls. The shrill voice feels like an arrow between my ears.

"This is it," I think, and expect them to discharge her. When I tell this to Ralph, he is surprised at my panic.

"Without giving her time to adjust?" he asks. Later

that week, one of the kinder nurses, Bea, will use the same expression: "She needs time to adjust; her behavior is not rare," adding, "It's to be expected; might take a few weeks till she adjusts." I calm down and look forward to my mother calming down as well.

Meanwhile, they change her room. I apologize to her roommate. "I am so sorry about last night."

Her roommate is direct, even gentle. "I am sorry for her, but I have to take care of myself," she says. Her forefinger, in an uncontrolled nervous motion, taps her thigh, which is covered by a pale green flowered cotton dress. She turns to look out the window. We are all sorry.

My mother does not adjust. She is put on drugs until they are afraid she will fall. She wanders away from the grounds. I'm called down by the nurse in charge, and find my mother, tied in a Posey, a harness-like restraint, at the nurses' station. So much for the Garden of Eden. I wonder what Shoshana would say now.

The nurses yell at my mother as though she has committed a crime. "We caught her going out the door," one says. Then, talking as if she isn't sitting right there, they agree:

"She's not like the others."

"She's never foolish."

"She always makes sense."

And I am no better than her new wardens. "Didn't you say you wouldn't do it this time?" I say, as if she had stolen something. When she doesn't defend herself, I am ashamed for not taking her side when she really needs me. My mother sits glowering, her spirit as restrained as her body.

A day later, I wait while my mother eats her meal in the dining room. She walks out, and I run to kiss her.

"Hello, Momma, how was lunch?" I ask.

"Very good, we had fish, vegetables and potatoes, a little fruit for dessert -- very good." Very good, I think, she remembers it all.

"They cook like you, Mom?"

"I'm not cooking and it was very good, very good."

The crowded corridor is bright with sunshine, and I am pleased, thankful. A resident walking behind me taps me on the shoulder.

"Your skirt is so beautiful," she says. "I always liked that color. I love pink."

"Thank you, so kind of you to notice," I say a little too loudly, hoping to establish the personal connection my mother and I are both hungry for.

At the very moment I turned away from my mother, I suddenly realize, she has walked into someone's room. Hers is around a corner, a considerable distance away.

I use the time for another lesson: "Ma, this isn't your room. Yours has the picture on the door." But she is beyond lessons, not hearing me, she stands in front of the dresser's mirror, comb in hand, quite at home.

And then, I hear the voice:

"Don't come in again . . . ." Her tone low and even,

the room's occupant's threat is cloaked in the gentility
Sunnyside Lodge prides itself on.

Because I have admitted to myself that my mother
has become addled, mildly senile, I believe that I am
accepting her condition. I know that she shouldn't be
walking into others' rooms. And I see the clouded look in
her eyes, and hear the fear in her voice, yes mildly senile.

There should be no terror in it, I tell myself. Senility
actually means "old," and she is at least 88 years old. It
will be six months before I understand that my mother's
behavior is symptomatic of dementia, a specific
degenerative disease.

Articles in newspapers and magazines publish
information -- cold facts -- on geriatric health issues daily.
Short segments are shown on television. It's easy to push
the paper away or turn off the set, and for the past year I
did. The media's very distance serves as a shield and
leaves out much of the story. The intensity in my mother's
blank stare cannot be communicated.

But now I begin to read ferociously; I know these
articles are about my mother's brain. The facts are that
the brain deteriorates differently for different reasons:
injury, small strokes, overmedication, infection, and more.

Other articles will tell me that there can be as many
as 100 causes for the same symptom. To make matters
even more complicated, medications needed for another

problem might be incompatible with those needed for dementia and cause harm.

As I watch my mother, I see that her symptoms are sporadic and mild: she wanders, compulsively sorts through drawers, and is confused about place. If a cause were to be determined, many of these symptoms could be reversed or at least mitigated.

Alzheimer's accounts for 50% of dementia. Alzheimer's patients are belligerent, the way my mother is, though this is the way she has always been. A stroke victim forgets and knows that he is not remembering, while Alzheimer's patients excuse their lapses, a symptom called confabulation. My mother, aware of her memory loss, claims that a fall on her head, a few years earlier, is responsible. This may actually be the case. Rummaging through her papers I have since found a victim's form, indicating that she was entitled to some compensation.

In addition, her circulation is also bad (intermittent claudication); an ophthalmologist explained that it had affected her vision. This condition probably contributes to her dementia as well. These are the facts of my mother's case.

Whatever the causes, and whichever kind of dementia she has, she is in its early stages. As a victim of the disease, she cannot control certain behavior -- the wandering, the confusion. I will learn that psychotic behavior is not an uncommon component of dementia, particularly when the person moves to a new setting.

Usually doctors and nursing homes don't take the time to learn what the cause is. Attitudes toward her behavior might be softer if a diagnosis were made. None was ever considered in my presence.

But the nurses at the Lodge must know that she cannot help herself. They should help me understand that her behavior is part of a disease, and prepare me to anticipate its symptoms and progression. But they don't! The staff is dishonest (except for Bea) -- especially when they imply that she is the exception. Sunnyside Lodge is working out much worse than I had imagined it could.

Hysterically, I call Karen Schwartz, the social worker at Morningside House (a nursing home I am interested in), terrified that my mother will be forced to leave the Lodge. I cannot look for a new place and take care of her at the same time.

Karen Schwartz advises that rather than wait for "the hammer to drop," I should initiate the action. Let the director, John Edmond, know that I am aware that my mother is extra work, that I will hire a full-time aide until she adjusts or until there is an opening in a more appropriate setting. She also tells me that legally they cannot put her out and gives me the names of other homes I may consider. Then Karen advises me, in a phrase I have used many times since, "Put your emotions aside," and do the practical work: fill out the applications for those other nursing homes.

It makes sense -- but how does it work? It's not

trading the pain for a constructive task, as one does with a dress that's the wrong size. Like a block of ice -- no carved angel gracing a buffet table -- I am paralyzed and chilled. Yet, I dial numbers and answer forms at a frenetic pace, like a gushing stream -- the water a vein of clarity racing down a mountainside. Are there two of me? Sometimes I wonder if someone else is doing the work. Amazed at myself, I learn to use my anxiety productively.

My meeting with John Edmond is quite formal, although in the past we've joked at the latest sitcoms and occasionally met in town, shopping.

I appeal to him on behalf of her last days, bargaining for compassion, reminding him that my mother and her room-mate are strangers sharing intimate space though they have never chosen to live together. He softens, though I know he wants her out. I also tell him that I understand that the Lodge is a community and that I am looking for another place in case she does not make the adjustment.

Luckily, I find Joan Dalalla, who works a twenty-four hour shift, four days a week. I relieve her for three of those hours and have to arrange for substitute aides on weekends. None of them have Joan's patience or understanding.

On the second weekend, despite our private aide, Ralph and I are awakened at 2 a.m. and told to come down and calm my mother. Ralph does it, reassuring her, validating her complaints. I stand numb, and become even more determined to find another place. Clearly, for her,

this one is wrong. Besides, including the wages for the
private aides, $125 a day, the cost is becoming prohibitive.

Joan is wonderful to me as well as to my mother.
She tells me how much she enjoys her. She says, "Your
mother is head and shoulders above these other women,
much more interesting," or, "There are others who do worse
things than your mother does." She is always reminding
me that my mother's behavior is not unusual there; she
assures me that many of the other residents wander as
well, but I do not know if those family members are also
called.

Together they talk about their lives, about religion,
about Joan's divorce although she's Catholic. My mother
had been a practical nurse, too, when she left my father. (A
year later, in a different nursing home, when a newspaper
article reports Ivana Trump's refusal to divorce because
she is Catholic, my mother remembers Joan: "Yes, it was
hard for my friend in that other place to divorce, hard to
do, but she did it.")

At the Lodge, Joan defends my mother: helping her
play Bingo, insisting that she be seated in the dining room
although the staff want her to eat alone with Joan. Joan
tells me how one night my mother pulled up her
roommate's blankets, thinking that she was caring for her
children. Her new roommate, Pauline, shrieked and
screamed. When the staff had complained to me about it, I
was sympathetic to Pauline. But Joan, who was there to
stop my mother and reassure Pauline, said Pauline was

putting on a show, said she caught her eyeing staff members in the room, "cool as a cucumber," and then started screaming as soon as they looked at her.

Joan is the only one who takes my mother's part in their territorial battles for the bathroom. At times Pauline locks herself up for as much as half an hour. These battles are intense; once my mother wet her pants.

Pauline had been the proprietor of a local gift shop and had been at the Lodge for fifteen years. She sits on a chair near the window, her legs spread apart, and plays with a piece of Kleenex, tearing it up and dropping it on the floor. Her physical needs are attended to, but, other than an occasional kind word, the staff does nothing for her. I was surprised when I heard her speak.

I have to spend three-hour shifts to relieve Joan, and I choose to spend that time at Sunnyside Lodge, thinking that my presence might help make the Lodge more comfortable for my mother. We practice finding her room; but even with the picture of a hat on the door to identify it she continues to wander into other residents' rooms. Finally, the stares are too much: both residents and staff smile at us for about a minute, and then stare as if we are all wrong. Soon, I have to get out, too.

There are errands to do. The fall brings a few windy days, so I take my mother to Morristown. There, we can buy gloves in a department store and do not have to walk as much as we would at the mall. My mother is quite particular about the gloves. Though she wants woolen gloves, she does not want them too heavy. "After all," she says, "I'm not a garbage collector; I don't work in the dirt," and shakes her head at me. I am a lost cause, no longer a New Yorker, or I'd know which gloves she wants -- and they have to be the right color. We settle on black.

Since my object is simply to kill three hours and not to accomplish anything, we never rush. On a warm day, we may go to the ice cream store in town, not just for ice-cream but because my mother enjoys the show. We watch parents patiently wait while their kids decide on what flavor they want. As she watches a three-hundred-pounder saunter out, licking a double scoop of chocolate ice-cream dipped in fudge and covered with jimmies -- and no apologies -- my mother comments, "Look, he knows what's good." Or we lunch at the local seafood store, which is always crowded with shoppers as well as diners; we often meet someone we know. Friends of mine live in town, and once or twice we visit in their back yard and watch the ducks float down the river. Her favorite stop, though, is with a friend's daughter, who has three little girls. On her deck, surrounded by pots of pink and red impatiens, the children buzz around us like fall bees. Danielle is four, and the twins are ten months. My mother revels in everything they do. Mostly she likes to watch them eat -- her eyes widen as the babies open their mouths, eager for the spoon glistening in mid-air.

We watch as the leaves change to yellow, then red and down to brown. Before this time, she'd brushed aside my exclamations about the leaves' beauty to review an argument in her New York life. But now, each time, she quotes the familiar lines I've heard growing up: "There isn't enough ink and there isn't enough paper to write the wonders of God's earth."

On rainy days I bring her to my house. Sometimes I fold laundry or pick-up. But by lunch-time, probably because of so many years of eating and cooking alone, she urges me to bring her back to Sunnyside so she can eat in its dining room.

We pass the time. Often the three hours are a chore, and I look at the clock, anxious to take her back.

IX

My Mother Had a Lover... A Hideaway

But, today I think about the time we have together. The sky is overcast, the air biting, raw, and the fall colors are particularly intense. I love days like these, which can be spent indoors or out. We decide to take a drive. Our doctor passes us on his bicycle. He has told me many times that my mother would not live out the year. He's been saying that for five years. When he waves from his bicycle, so light and free on this dark day, I think, "This year he could be right." Suddenly, I see my time with her as pure pleasure.

My mother acts changed too. She repeats my observations from yesterday's outing: how the children in the ice cream parlor chose their flavors, how friendly the people in the fish store were, what a wise choice the gloves have been, and she humors me about the fall foliage. It seems I've wanted her response to its splendor ever since I

moved to New Jersey. Possibly, she also feels this may be
her last year.

A day later, it is Indian summer. We drive down
Main Street, Boonton. Boonton's an old mining town. Its
Main Street -- a long steep hill -- is as much a time frame
as a place. For me it evokes the late forties, which is as far
back as I can feel a time. Its small shops, run by long-time
residents, sell specialty items: doll houses, costumes and
potters' art. There are florists, beauty parlors, shoe stores,
tailor shops and sport stores, the latter displaying pictures
of local sports teams and their trophies.

In the bright afternoon we park near the sidewalk in
my old Buick. It is hot -- the air-conditioning is not
working -- but we are protected from the glare of the day.
The dark brown dashboard and seats make the car feel as
though we are in a box, and the dark interior -- the
enclosed, sealed unit -- like a time machine, transports us
back to another time.

"Baruch didn't want to go . . . ," she says in a quiet
voice, not exactly to me.

"You mean . . . to Palestine," I say.

She nods and her thin arms press down against the
velour car seats, musty from New Jersey rains, the air
inside musty as well. We could be in an attic -- a place that
holds stored secrets. Her eyes search the sunny streets,
beach bright in their intensity. She pauses at shaded store
entrances, as if she expects to see Baruch Greenberg
emerge.

At first, Baruch's name seems to come out of
nowhere, which was often the case when I was growing up.
But today I think that the town's character may evoke her
earlier years too, and memories of him, which always seem
to make her happy and secure.

When I was growing up, she often talked about the
Greenbergs, Baruch's family, as if they were still next door.
Through the years, when she expressed an opinion, she'd
follow it up with, ". . . and Baruch laughed at them also,"
or, "Baruch laughed at the idea, that rich is better, so
foolish," or, "Baruch was angry at them." If she said, "he
laughed," she'd laugh, too. And even then, as a child, I
always sensed that the laugh wasn't for me.

Without warning, I find myself thinking about
Shoshana's visit last year. On that visit, I drove Shoshana
back to New York; her husband, Ariel, and my daughter
Laura were seated in the back. Suddenly Shoshana asked
me about Belva Plain's novel *Evergreen*.

She had sent it to my mother a few years earlier.
Though I had read the book, I'd always thought of it as
sentimental and loaded with clichés. I did not understand
why she wanted my mother to read it. My mother had
refused to read the book.

"I don't need other people's stories, anymore," she
had said then.

Other than its theme of the Jewish immigrant
experience, I didn't identify with it. It had all the
ingredients of a melodrama: the rendezvous, the illicit

affair, and the out-of-wedlock child. So when Shoshana asked me about the book, during the drive, I told her why I didn't like it, and she agreed, adding, "But clichés are often true . . . and a character and your mother . . . ," she had said. Then she stopped. For a hushed moment, she glanced back at her husband and Laura. That hesitation gave me the opening to ask her something, something I did not think I would have dared to consider before. The thought, a vague impression, had hovered in the air, like a scent that lingers once a person leaves a room. Now, I thought, now I will learn . . . .

"I wondered if . . ." I started to ask.

"For another time," she said, ending the conversation she had started.

The next day I was in the city and decided to call, hoping to meet with her. I had even bought her a copy of Cynthia Ozick's latest book. I asked her, "Maybe we can meet, yesterday you said . . . ." But she shushed me, "We won't talk about it. There is nothing to say."

Then the phone went dead.

"Nothing to say?" The words echoed in my head as I stood, stunned in the wings of the sidewalk phone. I would have flown to her to know . . . the connection could not have been more alive. "Nothing to say!" My mother and a character in a book? No, it was my mother and Baruch.

Once at home, I called my cousin Ann and asked her what she knew about my mother and Baruch, but did not mention my visit with Shoshana.

"Do you think there may have been something between Baruch and my mother?"

"Sure, that could have happened. Very possible," she had replied. I did not ask her any other questions.

When I told Ralph about our conversation, he also thought that my mother and Baruch might have had an affair, and then added, "Probably Ariel told Shoshana to let it be," adding, "I agree."

But I tucked the thought away.

*   *   *

Now my mother is the only one of the four still alive: Baruch, Monya, and my father have died. Relaxed, free from the tensions of Sunnyside Lodge, weakened by the heat, we drive past the shoemaker shop, when the big neon shoe in the front window nudges another memory.

"And when he went to the shoemaker's . . . ," she says, as she slowly turns her head away from me -- she is there -- ". . . he gave Baruch my shoes . . . ," and then, "No one was ever sure who belonged to who." I think she is laughing at how the merchant saw the immigrants: always together, a bouquet of wild flowers, jabbering in their own language. Then I think, no, she means something else.

But she has more to tell.

"He was going to get an apartment -- for us," she says, and now she is looking at my face, her hand slapping her chest, as she tells me this about herself and Baruch.

I begin to understand. So is that how it was: a hideaway? I cannot swallow the words -- "a hideaway." It's true, I'd never seen my parents as a romantic couple -- they were not like my friend's parents -- and yes, the idea that there was something between her and Baruch was not entirely new. But I had never imagined the details.

I had never pictured a hideaway. It was a story that sweetened a harsh life. With all the talk of "the closeness," I had never considered this. I was stunned with the suddenness I felt when Shoshana's silence had confirmed a hazy impression. How had she hidden it from me all those years?

I see my father's rage explode. I hear the accusations I thought he had invented: my mother running around with men -- impossible! I had never considered that he might have had cause. Still, I am relieved -- happy to know -- to really know. Now I know how it was. Thank God and bravo!

*   *   *

Sitting in the heat, on this summer afternoon, the picture of love-romance-intrigue comforts me. I ask no questions. What a relief, what an escape from the state we are in! It would make me happy if I had thought to invent it. I put my arms around my mother's bony shoulders. She smiles; a private smile, lips sealed. Our eyes do not meet.

I remember then that from time to time, even before Shoshana's visit, a breeze-like murmur would hint at more between our parents than the neighborly friendship my mother had described.

A particular scene comes to mind. It was after my

brother's death, a close friend and colleague of his visited my mother. As he spoke, seated across her in the dim shadows, her white head bowed under the lamplight, she turned to me, a faint smile on her troubled face. "He's just like Baruch," she said about my brother's friend.

The friend looked to me for an explanation. "An old lover," I had said without thinking. That was the first time I had said these words aloud. I don't know why I said them. It didn't register, not even with me, nor did I think about it again. My brother was dead. Nothing else mattered at that time. That a bereaved mother once may have had some joy, a romance, was a relief. I did not picture an actual affair.

How could I have known? As a child, I thought she was pretty when she dressed up. But mostly she cooked and cleaned, cream on her face and her hair in pin curls: I saw only a mother, the person who tried to fatten me up with bread and butter, warm milk, egg yolks in my cocoa.

But I do remember how my mother's passion and energy were impressed on everything she did. A friend, looking at some old photos, responded to those qualities. He said, "She sure was a sexual animal . . . even though it's usually said about men," and he held on to the photo, mesmerized. There was no décolletage; it was mostly her eyes. He had seen it immediately through the photos. I took much longer.

Once, when we were cooking dinner together in my

kitchen -- the children were out with their friends, at soccer practice, shopping -- she told me about a friend of hers, a trip that friend had taken, and then casually mentioned that woman's affair. I, who had always thought the husband was so nice, suggested there were things I probably didn't know, something that kindled the affair that justified the friend's betrayal of her husband.

"No," my mother assured me, "an affair can happen. It's not because something's wrong with your husband. It just happens," and she tossed her chin out making it clear that she knew what she was talking about. Yes.

And here she is, so frail. Seated with her in the hot car, I think how the revelation, not meant to be shared, slipped out like a treasured brooch she'd saved and polished. Her face softens as she thinks back to Baruch's scheme for a place of their own. She appears enraptured, her eyes glazed, like the afterglow of sex.

She is leaning against the car door and brings to mind a picture I had seen of her when she was a young girl, in a studio, sitting at that same angle: the brown car seats are like the photo's sepia background; the lines on her face fade into the photo. She wears a loose chiffon dress, her body is relaxed and sensuous; a languid aura floats out of the flat washed-out surface of the picture. In the hot car, she sparkles with a joy not diluted by nostalgia. She appears so set in the past that my looking at her makes me feel like an intruder.

Sitting there in the steamy heat, I recall the many stories she'd told about him. I try to compose Baruch and his family, and, like a mirage, settings appear as real as if I had been there. I imagine overstuffed chairs, big furniture, a white tablecloth on a heavy square dining table with ornate carved feet, a rose patterned rug, china with flowered patterns, black bookcases with glass doors. I can smell the cigarette smoke, and hear Yiddish being spoken. And yes, the men in white shirts. One, thin, wearing round wired glasses sits back on his chair, at the head of the table. Where had I seen it? Not in my house.

"He was going to get an apartment -- for us," she had said. So that is how it had been for her.

The car encapsulates us: Looking through the windshield, we go over old stories, moving in out of time and space, looking back when life had been good for her -- reminding me that she had had a life independent of mine.

A Different Mother

X

Life at Sunnyside Lodge / Morningside

The problems at the Lodge seem to matter less as we drive back after a day comforted by the past. My mother's revelation has made me happy, and I believe speaking about Baruch bolstered her spirits as well. But no sooner are we in the living room when Faith, a long-time resident, calls me aside.

"Maybe one day you can sit with her at the dining room table," she says.

"Oh, I never do that, I never go in the dining room."

"To help her . . . everyone tells her what to do and I think she gets confused. I mean, it's what she uses . . . she's mixed up." Faith pauses; she is having trouble telling this to me. "And then . . . and then she pours the milk and then the hot water and then the coffee . . . and she got it in the saucer . . . and then I was afraid she'd scald herself." When I say nothing, Faith adds, "And she spread the dessert custard on her vegetables." She takes a deep breath: "No, I'm not at the table. I see them all telling her what to do . . . it's too much . . . we try to help. I'm not complaining really; it's that I'm afraid she'll scald herself. So maybe you want to help her and just tell her . . . ."

"Thank you so much; you're so kind. I appreciate your interest but I could never tell my mother what to do: that would offend her."

The next day I take my mother out for lunch. She picks up a piece of broiled fish with her fingers. "Don't do that Mom, it's not nice . . . ." I don't stop, "It embarrasses me to see you do that." Fortunately, she does not stop or apologize.

Then, on Sunday, one of the private weekend aides says, as she polishes my mother's nails a bright red, "What a sad place this is. At Kessler's [a rehab center in West Orange, New Jersey] there's singing and children from the schools; here there's nothin'. I feel sorry for them." She is the first caretaker, except for Joan, who expresses any sympathy.

There is a lot of passive aggression at the Lodge: the help are often local women, who resent the residents' wealth. They appear unaware of the cruelties that old age itself inflicts. "Look at them, waiting already," they say, when a group lines up early, eager to play Bingo -- and they laugh together. Other activities also seem to be lacking in energy and understanding. I learn that one of the secretaries knows how to play the piano, so I offer to do secretarial work, to free her to play sing-along songs or light classics to lighten the place up a little. No, it isn't permitted. Occasionally, a resident may play. They do have a happy hour, where liquor is served, providing it doesn't interfere with their medication.

One woman will always haunt me: she is thin, neat; her gray hair is parted in the middle and arranged in a soft bun. She usually wears a tasteful silk dress and carefully placed jewelry. She takes a shot of whiskey and sits, her lips pursed, leaning on her cane, in total silence.

However, a chisel isn't needed to soften her stone-like visage. The staff is setting up a bachelor party for one of the young owners who is getting married. It takes almost an hour to gather everyone. Men lumber in, while women who'd spent years in wheelchairs -- their thighs as wide as table-tops -- wheel themselves in; others are escorted one way or another. A few strong enough to walk do not know where they are going. Then cookies and beverages are passed around. I cannot imagine what will happen next. A young blind resident plays a Chopin prelude on the piano. People nod, as if to say, "Isn't this nice?"

Then there's a scurry. A woman carrying a large square box with a handle, like a suitcase, goes to the center of the room. The man with her looks for an electrical outlet. The woman wears her coat, though it is quite warm. She lays a tambourine on the piano. Finally, she removes her coat, revealing purple harem pants and a sequined midriff. When the music starts from the phonograph she had brought, she slowly begins her dance, her veil teasing and taunting. As her torso undulates, a diamond in her belly button glimmers.

The audience stirs as well. The stone-faced resident responds, she tilts her head, her eyes brighten. Other faces surrender their flat medicated expression: a calcified place inside them has come alive. Aroused, the residents turn this way and that, slowly, sensuously shrugging their shoulders; invisible burdens fall away, and without a word they show they've known pleasure. My mother doesn't look at me. Her eyes are on the dancer. She, too, is transported.

Even the staff, so engrossed in the performance, is caught unprepared for the residents' response to it. Soon a few staff members look away from the dancer and point to someone who is usually dour or withdrawn. What pleasure! But since there is only one son, one bachelor party, the Lodge cannot have afternoons like this often.

Although the staff works hard, dressing, washing, bathing, weighing, running, doing what has to be done, they seldom smile or listen to the residents. One day when Joan couldn't make it, one of the aides complained, "Now I have to dress her!" She should have said, "Help dress her." Joan is starting to skip days, partly because her colitis is acting up.

"It's not your mother, believe me; I love her," she

says, "It's the staff. Let me take care of her at your house. I can't stand to be here."

Suddenly we don't have a choice. One day, my mother wanders off when I am late to relieve Joan. Two days later a person calls from Quiet Acres Nursing Home to tell me that Mr. Edmond has requested that my mother be transferred there. Quiet Acres is surprised that I know nothing about a transfer and that I am not agreeable to one. Our conversation is short, polite. Neither of us expresses an opinion about Mr. Edmond's unilateral decision. I had been to Quiet Acres and saw that everyone wore housedresses and sat in wheelchairs. It is livelier than the Lodge is, but I nearly choked on the smells, a mixture of medications and dirty wash water.

By now I've seen thirty homes. Amazingly, the costs are about the same in all of them ($90-125 a day, and most reserve a few places for Medicare). The Lodge charges extra for wheelchairs and medications and has no Medicare residents. One home asks for a year's payment in advance, $180,000. This place is highly recommended: "There are people there who function higher than your mother does," I am told. But I am overcome with its smell, a vomitus odor that seems to be breathed out in the enormous atrium that is packed with silent people. I think that if my mother were there -- no matter how bad she may get, no matter how she's lost reality -- in a moment's lucidity, a psychotic break would be the most appropriate response.

In another home, more than a hundred residents wander around a large bare room, six rickety aluminum tables and folding chairs lined up in its center the only furniture. Not a word is spoken. Not a sound. The social worker explains that, since it is after lunch, "They are sated." Another facility had placed four beds, almost touching in the middle of a room with a narrow aisle around them. I ask, if my mother goes here, could I pay for her to have either her own or a double room -- are there different rates? What about paying for a room as opposed to admitting her through Medicare?

"No, she would have to take the first available bed. Actually, they like the feeling of community," the social worker says, looking me straight in the eyes.

In another, where there is hardly any smell, I am told, "But she has to know how to work the remote for the television for when she's bedridden."

A few are not all that dismal. At Morris View Home, a county home with an excellent reputation, a gentle woman seeks to reassure me and kindly describes benefits my mother would have there: how, besides being fed and protected, she would be matched with someone she could get along with. I can tell they care, but at this time I am not allowed to see the facility, since they require a year's residency in the county before anyone is admitted.

By now my heart is set on Morningside House. There, when a grumpy man wheels himself into the elevator, a nicely dressed resident explains to fellow passengers, "He's agitated." That simple explanation decides it. The bustle of activity is not limited to the glittering covey that literally swarms all over the place: staff, volunteers, and visitors. The residents also have places to go to, and, as important, understand each other. This kindness in the elevator gives me a sense of the tone of Morningside House.

*   *   *

My mother has been in Sunnyside Lodge for six weeks. They give us a refund for the two weeks left in the month, which they are not required to do. With all the extras, wheelchairs, oxygen, medications, her six weeks there (not including our private aides) came to almost $8,000. As I write the checks I see her savings dwindle; there is little left. But they are so happy to get rid of her ("a belligerent woman," John Edmond had said) that they bend the rules. I want my mother to stay at my house for a month, till Thanksgiving. She likes Joan, and Joan is eager to work at my house. We schedule Joan to work during the days.

We find that is not so simple. At Sunnyside Lodge my mother leaned on Joan, whom she recognized as her protector. At my house she acts as if Joan is an interloper, coming between us. She does not let me talk on the phone, or shower, or do anything else alone. She moves to where I am, pushing me and holding me. Often I hang up the phone, give up the shower, put down my coffee cup and hold her, hug her, but that is not what she wants. She

111

wants to use my body as her own, and who can blame her?

As difficult as the days are, they are easy in comparison to the nights. She gets lost on her way back to bed from the bathroom. I consider it lucky when she climbs into bed with us, even if I manage to doze, because then I can take her back to her bed. To create a path from the bathroom directly across the hall to her room, I line up the kitchen chairs, two on each side, for roughly three feet, to the bed she has slept in many times in the last twenty-five years. In the morning, I find her sitting on a cold wooden chair, exhausted, or, if she pushed the chairs aside, naked, eagle-spread on the living room couch, her rigid limbs at sharp angles; she is only sharp angles now, my mother, an old regal bird.

Fortunately, after three days there is an opening at Morningside House. Openings are based on severity of need, not merely on where you are on the list. To see if my mother qualifies for the opening we have to bring her there. Ralph comes to help, and my mother is curious and even-tempered. The truth is I've given her an extra melaril, to keep her so. My not-too-happy secret.

*   *   *

Morningside House, like Sunnyside Lodge, had also been a wealthy women's retirement home, where women once wore white gloves to four o'clock tea. The lobby, which opens to an attractive garden, is furnished with valuable antiques, as are the community rooms and occasionally some of the residents' quarters: Hitchcock originals and

Chippendales. Fine clocks are used in the community rooms on each floor, giving an aura of substance and quality. But here, when the residents began to fail, the care is modified to meet their needs. No one pretends that people stay the same, and thus changes in care are made (unlike Sunnyside) appropriately.

Karen Schwartz, the chief social worker, accompanies us on the tour, although that is not her usual obligation. I need her to intercede if my mother should complain or, worse, make a scene, although Cynthia, the admitting person, is also very helpful. We go to the fifth floor, where the residents are the most independent -- Related Care.

Ralph looks around. I understand his thoughts: "If only I had known about this for my parents." Certainly, I know this home is the best: everyone is kind, and my mother needs more care than I can provide. Yet, as Ralph and I stand together in the elevator on the way to the fifth floor, I feel my earliest memory rush over me.

I am in an enormous dark room; only one end is lighted. A polished granite floor, its squares of mottled stone delineated by gold strips -- possibly a dance floor in a synagogue, or its lobby -- stretches three hundred feet, maybe three thousand, and I am screaming as my mother, shrouded by the darkness, disappears.

That memory has always been so painful that I never tried to find out if she was leaving me for a long time -- when we were in the orphanage because of her broken arm, or later, in day-care, when she started to work in the factory. To ask her about it would have been to accuse her.

As the elevator door opens, I think, "Is this how you feel? It can't be helped now either." I wish I could fix both of our pains.

After the tour and the interview, Cynthia, the admissions director, tells us my mother has to move in on the following day. I am both surprised and relieved when my mother agrees. A secretary walks across the lobby to tell her that she is welcome at Friday morning religious services that week.

"And if I don't want to come to services?" my mother asks.

"I will be singing there. It will be nice," says the secretary, a heavy woman who looks fiftyish.

Again, my mother rejects her: "So if you sing, I have to listen?"

"My voice is not so strong," she says, indicating her girth. "Besides, there is a very worthwhile woman there whom I want to introduce you to." This she says in Yiddish.

I want to tell her that my mother speaks English very well, and also that she is as resistant as they come and not to be insulted by her.

But my mother softens, her value has been acknowledged.

"I would very much like to meet her," she says.

An older man, a volunteer, comes over, and says

hello, and adds, "You are a very nice looking woman."

"I'm not so nice looking," she answers.

"But you're not homely," the last phrase he too says in Yiddish. My mother nods in agreement: this, she would not argue.

She thanks Cynthia and Karen for their time and attention and agrees to stay there. She agrees that it is a nice place, and admits that the people are okay.

The car ride back is quiet, though Ralph takes a wrong turn and has to retrace his tracks. Once we get home, she asks,

"Don't you think, maybe we should look a little more, maybe some place closer?"

Up until this point, Ralph understood that I had to work at the job of finding a nursing home for my mother my way, even though he thought I was overdoing it. He knows I still want to defer to her. By now we are all in the kitchen, having eaten dinner in a diner. We are standing in the twilight, and have not turned on any lights. The flame-colored countertops are dulled, except for slashes of sunlight that steal through the windows.

While Laura makes tea for her, my mother hovers over it. Laura says, "A watched pot never boils, Nannawanni," and my mother answers, "So, get another pot."

"Not so funny," Laura says. Laura and I nod. We are in agreement: Yes, we need Morningside House.

Again my mother asks, her two hands around the

cup of hot tea, "Maybe we should look a little more?"

Respectfully and patiently Ralph explains to her that this time we have to make the decisions -- even if we are wrong, although he assures her he does not believe that to be the case.

"Momma, Do you know how many homes Rena went to?" he asks. "She went to fifty. She, and me too, we want the best for you. We know how hard you worked, we love you Momma, we only want you to have good care."

He goes on to talk about our children, and how we had admitted to them that even if he might be wrong, being responsible he had to make the decisions, and that was now the case with her. "But I know we are not wrong. I know this is the best." He takes a breath . . . my mother smiles.

"I think you deserve an academy award," she says.

Our trip to the nursing home seems to go without a hitch. The day is bright and sunny, traffic is light, and we are all quite business-like. There are almost no leaves on the trees. Laura sits in the back with my mother, who voices no objections to her situation. Once we arrive at the nursing home, she says thoughtfully and gently, "Maybe we should take one more look for a different place. Let's go back to New Jersey."

"But my academy award?" Ralph asks.

She laughs...."Okay, okay, you win."

Despite my relief at discovering Morningside House,

I feel no victory. I am dreading another "adjustment" to institutional living, and for what? I see future time as one enormous humiliation. Not only will she get weaker and sicker, but also her confusion will be greater. Why extend the misery? I know she will die here. I am prepared for her death as she is being admitted. I want it. I want to avoid the interim pain. I do not expect her time at Morningside House to have a purpose. She has led a full and vigorous life. She has become a phantom. Of course she resists going, and I resist it, too.

Laura thinks back to that first night at the Lodge, and tries to warn Earl Collum, our new fourth floor social worker. He assures us, "We are experts at first nights. And she can leave; she can have Thanksgiving with you," he says.

At first I visit her three times a week, which means I go one day, rest the next, and so on. I am still not walking firmly on the ground, finding it hard to reconcile her vague confusion with the tough woman I have grown up with. When she is lucid, she is as bright as ever -- remembering old times, talking about family ties (although Baruch is not part of these conversations), and making jokes. On those days I am buoyed; on the others, when she does not remember that I am married, or that I live in New Jersey, I sink. Laura comes with me once a week and phones every day, saying all the right things, not correcting her as I do.

But her adjustment is hard in Morningside House too. She wanders into other residents' rooms, their beds,

117

their drawers. The residents are angry at her, although Mary, one of the nurses, is sure it is temporary, just a difficult adjustment for an independent woman.

"You know, she can't help it," she explains to the distraught residents.

"What are you looking for?" Mary has asked her.

"Yesterday," she answers.

XI

The Nicest One

David and Carol are supposed to pick her up from Morningside House on their way down from Boston for Thanksgiving dinner. They are already two hours late. Morningside has called a few times at my mother's request. Everyone is here -- Zach and Laura and their close friends, who are new to America: Alex from Russia; Kathy, brought up in Japan for much of her life; Claire from Ireland; Hsui, Carol's maid of honor, from Taiwan. By now most of the hors d'oeuvres are gone or cold, napkins crumpled, sparerib bones lying in dishes. I am afraid the turkey will be dry. The day is beginning with a familiar tension.

Finally, they are here; "There was so much traffic," Carol says, as she helps my mother unbutton her coat.

"Couldn't get out of Cambridge," David says.

I remember that it is the most heavily traveled weekend and notice that my mother is missing her bottom teeth. I also realize that her faithful apple pie is missing as well. But she is here for Thanksgiving, despite a visit to the hospital for heart congestion two weeks after starting at Morningside House, and I am thankful.

This urge of mine to have her at my house for Thanksgiving seems unreasonable: she has always complicated it. I was never sure whom she'd insult. Even so, despite all the attention she needs, it would not be Thanksgiving without her. My hope for a peaceful meal is not as strong as my need for her presence. Once, early in our marriage, Ralph, the babies, and I went to Florida for a much needed vacation. All I remember is missing Thanksgiving: the fussing and rushing, the sounds of dishes and people clattering, particular tastes and voices. All my senses were starved for it, and I decided I would never miss it again.

When we were children, we were the only ones in our neighborhood who celebrated Thanksgiving with a turkey and cranberry sauce. True, my brother was born on Thanksgiving and we were all at home on that day, but our celebration was more than convenience or coincidence: We felt this American holiday was ours, since it was not religious as were Christmas and Good Friday. And my mother argued that "America was good to us," meaning the Jews. She could still feel the brutality of Russian persecution and discrimination.

Ironically, the Thanksgiving holiday was stronger for us than Passover, a lunar holiday that could fall on a week day -- a work day that my mother could not give up to prepare the meal properly. On those Passovers we'd have dinner -- with a linen tablecloth and wine -- in the kitchen, without the ceremonial foods or reading of the Passover story -- not like the lavish Passovers my cousin Ann told me we once had. I vaguely recall once going to a relative's, arriving late, and--although welcomed--feeling extraneous, as if I'd entered into a movie that had already begun.

Thanksgiving was clearly our family holiday, but no relatives were invited. I'm not sure if it was because my parents weren't on speaking terms with any of them, or if everyone lived so far away -- too far to ask them to make the trip to our modest apartment. Instead, each of us children invited a friend. We'd open up a table in the living room, dress up, and enjoy the pure American menu -- capped off with my mother's wonderful sour cream cookies and apple pie. My father would smoke a cigar. I remember the Russel Wright dishes, the flowered drapes, but do not remember any tension then. Even now, the smell of a cigar evokes those dinners and scenes of contentment.

After my sister and I married, Bernice made Thanksgiving at her big house in Westchester. Her husband, who was part Cherokee, wore an Indian headdress that reached down to the heels of his shoes. My parents, who had been unhappy with Bernice's marriage, had separated by then, and only my mother came. My sister is an excellent cook, and my mother did not mar her talent, and the glorious meal, with any other observations.

Those Thanksgivings were fun, but six years later my sister divorced and moved to California. From then on, Thanksgiving has taken place at my house.

Tension was always a certain, though unwelcome, guest. Of course, being young and having to organize a festive meal for a big group could have been the reason I'd be nervous -- hoping the turkey would be tender enough, the house clean enough, the children behaving well enough -- and then having to please everyone while conflicting personalities waged their small battles.

The apprehension was justified: as soon as my brother, his wife, and my mother entered the house, its presence scratched, like eggshell in the mixing bowl. After a few hours in the car with my mother talking non-stop, my sister-in-law's pale face tottered on her long neck, literally gasping, as if my mother's talk had used up the oxygen.

Her coat off, my mother invaded the kitchen. She'd bring her pie dough; I'd supply the apples. Once she started rolling her pies, the flour flying, Laura would complain that she didn't want apple pies. It was not my mother's pies, but my mother's aggressiveness and open preference for my noisy free-wheeling boys that upset my daughter. In almost the same breath that she promised the boys a separate pie, one just for them, she might kiss Laura and ask, "You gained weight?" and then ask Laura if she had tried any new recipes from the Weight Watcher's Cookbook she'd bought her for her eleventh birthday.

Fortunately, this tumult was offset by my in-laws,

who came each year until they were too frail. My father-in-law brought his loving nature; though he could barely read, his grocery store provided modest vacations for his family and a fur coat for his wife. Both would spend the time adoring their grandchildren. My mother-in-law, though more restrained, doted on Laura in particular.

Others came and unknowingly acted as shields in the crossfire; shots would arise out of seemingly innocent comments. For example, one time my sister-in-law described her cat's antics, while my brother, who thought they were cute, was so allergic to cats that his eyes were always red and swollen. Then my mother said, as if she were asking someone to pass the salt, "If I was a good person, I'd kill the cat."

Another recurring issue was my brother's refusal to accept birthday presents. Once, my mother bought him opera tickets. He showed no mercy and made it clear that he didn't want her to impose her tastes on him, and invade his time; she should have known that, as much as he loved music, opera was the one form he hated.

Usually, Ralph invited a few foreign medical residents from his program at the hospital; they politely observed, "How lovely just to eat and talk, no presents." Our friends from town came for many years. Each year we'd include either old friends from Washington, or relatives. Although every Thanksgiving began with a clear caul of tension, we had fun as well.

Zach built a roaring fire (one year, a glass door on

the fireplace exploded). Bernice, with uncanny precision, always called from California just as a benign competition between our friend's pie and my mother's had begun. My sister-in-law napped on the couch. Simon might smoke a cigarette with Laura. We sang show tunes; a group would shoot baskets. Invariably, on leaving, my sister-in-law would say, "This was the nicest one."

But that all changed. My brother and his wife divorced, and he died shortly after. A new law limited foreign medical residents. My mother took the bus to our house until she was too weak, then came with Zach when he lived in New York, or I'd pick her up on the Wednesday before. I had told David to weigh the long trip from Massachusetts against his studies -- assuring him that the holiday was not a command performance -- so he missed a few Thanksgivings.

My mother and Laura gradually moved toward rapprochement. She prepared tea for my mother, and was always sure to have a cube of sugar for her to hold in her teeth, sweetening the hot liquid as she drank it.

Today, we have come full circle. Only the children's friends are here. Tension has been converted to deference for my mother as she allows herself to be led tenderly from couch to chair. When Alex sits on the hassock of my mother's chair, they speak Russian, Alex reciting from a book of Pushkin's poetry while she adds lines she knows from memory.

Soon we are all cozy in front of the TV watching a

short video of Carol and David's wedding this past summer. Crowded and lazy, some of us sit cross-legged or sprawled out on the golden shag rug under the soft lights. I am fussing with the remotes, to start the video. The wood-burning stove keeps us extra warm. Zach, feeding the fire, calls to her:

"Nannawanni, now you'll be nice and warm."

She answers, "In Russia I had such a stove."

"And your father chopped the wood . . . " (this exchange has taken place before -- many times).

"And I carried it in the house . . . I did." She is so proud. (I remember her adding, ". . . and I carried in the water from the well." I am amazed how her slightest shrug replays tapes of her life in my head.)

My mother had been at the wedding and led the procession down the aisle, but the video confuses her. She takes in faces brushed by summer breezes on the screen, then turns to those same faces before her. She reaches out to David and softly strokes his cheek. They exchange smiles, and he holds her hand, caressing the thin bony fingers, as he enjoys his wedding day on the TV screen. There, green leaves shimmer. The house we sit in smells of garlic, turkey, and fresh-baked cakes. Outside the windows, branches bereft of leaves sway.

Like my mother's, my eyes are not on the TV either. I scan the room, enjoying the pleasant disorder -- cracked chestnut shells in small bowls, TV remotes on the floor, Ralph's open newspaper, David's shoes. I pause at the

pictures that hang on the walls: a Mary Cassatt print
portraying a dark-haired woman as she baths the feet of a
toweled five year old; the other, bought at a local fair, a
painting of a herd of prancing horses. I see my mother and
me: she is bathing me, and I am listening to her stories of
beautiful horses on the plains of Russia.

Kathy leans toward her and whispers that she and
Alex plan to marry in June. My mother knows they have
been together for five years. About their relationship, she
frequently said, "Without the law it can be stronger," and
referred to Anna Karenina's bond to Vronsky: "She gave
up society, even her child; she demanded more loyalty; they
demanded more from each other" . . . I hear the whole
mantra during that brief moment, when Kathy leans over
to tell her about her wedding plans -- soft lights and
shadows cradle the memory. I see my mother, her lips
sealed, holding the idea in her mouth. "It can be stronger,"
she had once said, but for Kathy she is all in the present.

"What . . . are you pregnant?" she asks, surprised
and delighted at the same time.

"No, no, no," Kathy assures her and practically lifts
my mother in an embrace. Then they dance in a circle, my
little mother suddenly spry and joyful, and now it seems
that the missing teeth somehow enhance, deepen, her
smile. She tires, her face is pale. Kathy kisses her once
more and Ralph gently leads her to our bedroom, where he
sits with her as she rests on our chaise.

Because of a Medicare thirty-day residency ruling,

my mother has to go back to Morningside House this night.
There are many kisses. Carol helps her on with her coat.
Laura brings a blanket for the trip back. In the car, Ralph
carefully places it on her lap. I do not envy him the drive,
and hope he'll be patient with her questions while he
battles the George Washington Bridge traffic.

I need not have worried. When he comes back (just
as we begin to clear the table, having gone over all the old
jokes we know), he is enthusiastic and describes a virtual
parade of adult children and their elderly parents,
welcomed by a staff member at Morningside House.

"Good evening, Mrs. Trefman. How was your
Thanksgiving? We have a cup of tea for you and some
buttered bread."

"Good evening Mr. Rossi, how was your
Thanksgiving? Is the new baby talking? We have some
cafe-au-lait and a piece of peach pie for you." Each resident
was welcomed by name, and their favorite evening snack
had been prepared. Ralph says, if he hadn't seen it, he
wouldn't have believed it.

Everyone is gone, and the house is quiet. I place the
leftover sweet-potato soufflé in the refrigerator and smile
to myself. Frail as she is, I understand that she has held
the day together. In their kindness to her I see my family
has grown up. They are kind to each other as well.
Surprisingly, even the turkey was extra tender. Everyone
seemed happy to be here; this Thanksgiving really was the
nicest one.

A Different Mother

XII

The Third Floor: Kindness in Abundance

Karen phones to tell me they are considering changes for my mother. "We may have to move her. The next time you come, drop by the office," she says. "Don't worry, she's fine."

I do worry and visit the following day. The length of the trip and the harrowing bridge and truck traffic wear me out. I feel so defeated I can accept almost anything. And I have to.

"Hi," Karen greets me with her usual warm smile. She urges me to take a seat and with no other preliminaries tells me how things are.

"Rena, we decided to move your mother to the third floor. We've had zillions of meetings, arguments, but she is surrounded by so much anger -- the residents, not the nurses," she assures me, "that we thought it would be better. Mary keeps saying that she just needs more time.

But we (she means the administration) feel that she should have made the adjustment by now. It's been over a month. Quite honestly I agree and think she'll be happier."

There is very little space for me to say anything. The office is small, but the tightness is in my throat. I try to imagine my mother on the third floor where the residents are all very confused and disoriented. I think, maybe I could get someone like Joan. I worry that she might sink faster without the restraining presence of the fourth floor residents, who act like regular people. My mother has always been a free spirit with little regard for the feelings of others. What has kept her in line is her inordinate pride.

I am somehow offended that others think she needs to be on the third floor. "Is she so bad?" I ask myself. I know she will receive more attention from the staff, and less anger from the residents, when she wanders into their rooms, their beds, their drawers.

The move accomplished, I visit two days later. The third floor makes no demands, and my mother is more comfortable. It is not unusual for residents to nap in someone else's room. I see a woman wearing a blouse, a bronze print that is unmistakably my mother's -- I am not happy about that. My mother, in the spirit of the third floor, says, "A manufacturer makes more than one. So she chose the same blouse! So what!"

There is still some contact with the fourth floor. Friday morning, sometime after my mother had left it, a woman approaches her at religious services. She winds her way close to my mother and asks, "Do you remember me? Anna, do you remember me?"

Stunned at how my mother is failing before my eyes, grateful that she knows me, I ask, "Eva, why do you think she can remember you?"

"I want her to remember that I was good to her," she says. It was true that not everyone on the fourth floor was. But the flood of kindness somehow does not make it easier for me. My mother has always been too proud to accept kindness: she thought it too close to pity. Now, I am finding it hard to accept too, because it emphasizes what is happening to my strong, independent, passionate, bright mother. I know that at her age it happens that this decline is the human condition, like a two-year-old's baby talk. I try to convince myself that her condition is normal. I try to accept it because she was not defeated, but believed her life was victorious. And also because now I know she loved freely.

There is a difference in her behavior. She is not simply forgetting. Her sense of time and place is erratic. Because of her sudden short term memory loss -- not remembering where her room is, or not remembering the aide who'd just spoken to her -- I understand that my mother is probably afflicted with Alzheimer's like many others who are on this floor. But it is mild, I say to reassure myself, she is still one of the best on the third floor, and I am proud of that. At the same time I know that pride would not be my response if she were in the early stages of cancer or diabetes.

I am learning that Alzheimer's is a physical condition, that there are brain changes -- "tangles" which are composed of twisted nerve fiber, and "plaques" which consist of dead or dying cells surrounding a substance called beta amyloid -- and that the longer one lives, the more likely it is that this deterioration will occur. Nevertheless, a shadow of shame interferes with my accepting the symptoms of Alzheimer's as a disease. Somehow I cannot give up the feeling that if she would only try harder she'd remember and would not say such odd things.

She is beginning to ask to see people who have died. But not a word about Baruch. I wonder if he's been banned from Morningside House, if he is welcome only to places that the young and healthy Anna remembers, or places like Main Street, Boonton, that remind her of those days. She asks to see her mother most of the time. Today, after repeated requests for her mother, which I do not acknowledge, she looks into my eyes, checking to see if she is reading me correctly, and asks,

"We can't see Momma?"

I heave a sigh of relief, "That's right, ma."

"The car's broken," she says to explain it.

It's taking me a long time to know that she cannot accept my explanations. And I promise myself to stop correcting her. All along, Laura knows how to respond.

When my mother wants to see my brother, Laura might say how sweet Simon was, how she had loved him, and then gives her the information that he died.

"Really, what happened?" She asks as if she hadn't visited him in the hospital or gone to the funeral.

As Laura speaks, a memory of Simon washes away my sense of him as the sardonic professor, the 18th century English literature specialist I knew in his adult life. I see a young boy and myself -- a pesty seven year old -- in the disorganized railroad flat we lived in, in the East Bronx....

One Saturday morning, the beds are unmade, I am busy tormenting him. Simon is about twelve -- too tough to bother with me. I slap him and run. When that doesn't get a response, I grab his comic book -- running away with it, jumping on the unmade beds. When he finally grabs it back, the cover tears. "I got it, you little bastard," he says uncharacteristically.

Immediately, I proudly report my response to Simon to my mother, reciting very confidently, "Ma, I told him, 'Maybe Bernice was a bastard, or maybe you were one,' I told him, 'but by the time they had me, they had to get married. '" I feel so smart and my mother seems to enjoy the story.

"Well," she says, turning to the stove, lowering the gas; the flame, a luminous blue fringe quivers like little breaths under the busy aluminum pot. Her eyes smile. Then she adds, "I could have gone to someone else."

While that challenged my bravado and gave me

something to think about, I didn't quite get it. I wonder now what slight calibration makes this scene emerge so clearly from the abyss of my memory. And I am shocked at the clarity. I see her smile; I see it form even though she has turned away from me. I see the tilt of her head and how her black hair, set away from her widow's peak falls in a generous wave, framing the left side of her face. As little as I was, I see the neckline of her tiny-flowered pale blue print cotton dress. I even note that it was fall, sun dappled on exposed sheets. I don't remember ever thinking about this before.

There is so much going on here, I put the questions aside, pressing the memory back, burying it in tangles of my "healthy mind."

"Later," I say to myself, "later."

I look at poor mama, all mixed up, but know that she is not always lost or sad, and, when she is lucid entertains the staff with stories of her childhood in Russia. They not only listen, but encourage her and pass her stories on. She often sings a song about America:

> *America is a golden lond*
> *Keiner veist nit fun kine shand*
> *A koimen-chera vert a president.*

> America is a golden land,
> No one knows from any shame
> A chimney-sweep can be a president.

"Come on Anna, this is the 1990's, this is New York!!" Caren Taylor, a nurse, says. "We don't have chimney-sweeps; do better!" and my mother tries. She sings,

> America is a golden land
> No one knows from any shame
> A...a... PROSTITUTE can be a president.

"Now you're talking, Anna," Caren Taylor says. My mother is at ease, and begins "to adjust."

I am making adjustments too, learning to look at and judge her life at Morningside House differently than life in the world outside. Long before, when Ralph's mother was in a "home," I had told the children that I didn't want them to visit me when I became that way, not to run as he did to a woman who barely knew her son. It was not only because I wanted them to enjoy life, go to baseball games and such, but because I was afraid that they would remember me that way -- weak and sad, not railing against them in the kitchen, in charge.

"Don't visit me," I would insist.

"Mom, you don't know what you'll want when you're 'that way.' Then you'll have only moments," David said, adding, "and I hope I will be able to make many of them happy." I was ashamed of myself.

Now the time has come when my mother is "that way." I see how urgent her "moments" are, as David said they would be, and I learn that her life is active as well, though I have adjustments to make as soon as the elevator door opens.

135

Dora, a new resident meets me there. A heavy, pale woman in her late seventies, her clear hazel eyes notice everything. Dora, who has been here for only a few months, and has never known my mother before, explains each time, "You know, we've been friends for a long time, many years, from the building." I can tell by her expression, her arched eyebrows and broad smile, that Dora recognizes me, although I have to introduce myself each time. Sometimes, I give her a Hershey chocolate kiss.

In the afternoon, as I am leaving, I bump into her son. He looks distraught. He has been getting used to her situation, so I wonder if anything untoward has happened. I learn that he is upset because his brother never visits -- an old story at nursing homes.

"I don't mind what she calls your mother, or Rose," (another woman on the floor) he says, "if she calls them her children, her nieces and so on, she feels needed, and they do answer her need."

"Oh she is needed," I reassure him. "She makes a very big difference in my mother's life."

"I know that, I know that, and I'm glad. All my friends say that as long as she's happy I shouldn't feel bad. But I do, and then my brother doesn't come; he just doesn't care."

"Maybe it's painful for him," I say, allied with the son I've gotten to know, since I, too, am the only child taking the responsibility for my mother's well being (although my sister is really too far away to be involved).

"I understand it's classic. Maybe if we weren't here . . . they'd . . . ."

"No," he interrupts, "as long as she's fed and has a place to sleep, he's satisfied, but I know she'd like to see him. You know, that woman ran a full office floor -- an office that was on the New York Stock Exchange . . . and now . . . ."

"She's still running the floor, Al. It's just a different floor," I say.

It's true. If a resident walks around without shoes, Dora finds a nurse and yells, not stopping until the nurse or aide puts the shoes on. At night she takes a group of residents and lays them down in her bed. She guards her door, to protect her weaker friends -- her treasured antiques -- while an aide or nurse tries to get them to their own beds. Once, she intervened when a man came to see his mother: "She has to sleep now," she said to the son and would not let him enter the room. They say she is trouble. Maybe that is true. But she is also a blessing.

My mother is sent to a nearby hospital because she had a mild stroke. As soon as I enter the room, she asks to see her dead relatives: her mother, her sister, my brother. Then, she asks for "Esther." I sense she means Dora, and decide to phone the nursing home. I am right.

Once they are on the phone, speaking Yiddish, I only get her side of the conversation, and soon hear my mother say that I am there, boring her to death. When Dora talks, my mother listens; her eyes glow and she chuckles with pleasure.

Once back in the nursing home, although my mother is still on the third floor, she sits at a table for those who need help feeding themselves. She no longer goes to the special activity program. I think her friendship with Dora is over. They do not see each other in the same place or way.

One day, in the Rose Garden, I bring them together. My mother, seated in her wheelchair, looks up at Dora, beaming. Dora bends down, takes my mother's face in her hands, and kisses her.

I am learning that Morningside is a real community, and that there are many friendships like Dora's and my mother's -- friendships alive with insults as well as kisses. On the fourth and fifth floor there are marriages as well.

Many of the residents belonged to the International Ladies Garment Workers Union, as my mother did. When I was a child, I went for fittings at the factory, where my mother and her fellow workers pooled their labor, sewing coats for me and other relatives. Though their bantering was loud and rough -- double entendres filled the air -- I was comfortable there and enjoyed their pride. So it is particularly jarring for me to hear the doctor at Morningside House assuring a resident that there is no charge for his consultation. He means well, as he repeats, "It's free," with a friendly smile. The woman fumbles with her empty pocket book. He repeats a few more times, "It's free." Bending down, I whisper, reminding her that she has paid her taxes and worked hard: She belonged to the union, now the government and the union will pay the medical bills. She sighs with relief, "Thank you, I forgot, thank you for telling me," she says, her shoulders squared.

The mix of residents is so varied. One (on the fifth floor) had been a director in charge of communications for a major company. He MC's the weekly professional entertainment, usually music -- folksy, brash, or classical -- violins, opera, singers, sing-along, dancers in beautiful costumes, or story-telling. And the entertainers touch, visit and often embrace the residents.

Or there's Dave, a former attorney, decked up in a bow tie, seated in his wheelchair (in addition to advanced Alzheimer's, he's also lost a leg to diabetes), who always greets us with, "Hi beautiful," or "Hi doll," though I am not sure if he recognizes us from one time to the next.

His brother, a big heavy man close to seven feet tall, comes often, tenderly bending down to listen, making sense of his disparate references. To liven up his day, Dave's brother hired Angela, pert and vivacious, for a few hours each afternoon.

Angela talks to the other residents, dances for them, hugs them, brings them juice and listens to them. She tells me their stories: Ben had been a watchmaker, his only visitor a woman he'd employed in his jewelry store when she was abandoned as a young mother. Doona, 95, stooped and nearly blind, with a little beer from her son, dances

Irish clog-dancing. Docile Mike, handsome and genteel,
may have been a hit man for the Mafia. Angela explains
that Kathleen cannot stop crying, no matter how hard the
staff tries to comfort her, because her daughter's getting a
divorce.

Angela tells me she loves my mother very much and
repeats their conversations. She says she understands why
now my mother expresses a wish to die, "because she loved
life so much." I wonder how Angela sees that in my
wizened mother, and how she senses her daring in love.

At Morningside House, somehow, each person's
essence, even meanness, is ferreted out, appreciated, as an
act of life.

On the afternoon Helen's lunch was not delivered,
Carla, a staff member, calls for it. She tells Helen it is
coming.

"I'm hungry, I want my lunch," Helen says.

"It's coming." Carla assures her, a few times. The
others tell her to quiet down and let them eat in peace.

"No, I'd feel just like Helen, hungry, having to sit
and watch everyone else eat," Carla says, "I'd want to yell
too." Validated, Helen waits quietly.

A resident's relative yells at a staff member. I feel so
bad and embarrassed for her, especially because I know
how dedicated she is. She smiles when our eyes meet.

"They're nervous and upset," she says to me. "You
know, to see him that way."

It has taken time, but I have learned not to be afraid

of the residents, their grotesque behavior, the aimless walking, their attempts to undress themselves, the crying, and the casual smooching between a man and a woman. As dedicated as most relatives are, some, including staff from other floors, cannot face that graphic embodiment of human deterioration.

At first, I go to Morningside House's six-week evening program for residents' families only so the social worker will know me and listen when I complain. Instead, I learn to make sense of the third floor. My terror subsides.

Luther, Belle's son, teaches me the most at these sessions. "Join in, take part," he says. When he visits his mother, he helps feed mine, he jokes with her, asks her questions and listens to her answers.

My mother belongs here. Possibly one day I might, too, and still be valued. Nevertheless, isolation and despair are persistent visitors. Now, gingerly, guarded, so they don't get me, I prepare to do battle with them.

When Ralph's parents had been in a nursing home, some fifteen years earlier, I seldom visited them. I was busy with our young children, and, besides, he didn't want me to. During that time, we had taken a vacation at the ocean. A woman sitting on the beach struck up a conversation with me and said that she spent much of her time visiting her aunt and uncle in a nursing home. I told her I admired her to be able to do it and how awful I felt in my in-laws' nursing home the few times I did visit.

"Go more often," she said. "Go more often." I never expected to remember her; and then one afternoon my mother and I are talking, like old times, I think. I look at her in her wheelchair and see how tiny she has become, suddenly realizing that she is shrinking away. Then I see the scene, this strange woman sitting on a chair in the sand earnestly looking at me; I see her sitting before me, and hear her say, "Go more often," and begin to understand the enormity of my mother's last days.

XIII

The Rose Garden: Is He My Father?

"Come with me, Sophie," Laura says, her arm around Sophie's shoulder, "I want to show you something," and she points to a vase filled with flowers on the nurses' station. "Aren't they pretty?" Laura asks, and receives a soft hazy smile as a reply. The afternoon sun reaches through the dining room and settles on the aquamarine carpet. The usually dark hallway is now a sea of floating chairs.

I struggle to accept life on the third floor, while Laura has another perspective. She feels the third floor is where the truth is, and understands an eighty-year-old's longing for her mother or her dead son. She is not upset when she or my husband or I are suddenly reached for and held to make-up for the missing, "Moishele . . . Surah, Josephina," or "mommale." Or when just as suddenly, a blast of obscenities fill the air -- spittle flaring like crystal chips in the sun's rays.

I learn from my daughter as she quietly compliments a dress or haircut and tenderly leads the residents -- confused, sometimes ashamed, their poison purged -- from their painful ghosts. We are all learning, even my mother, who might mumble about her new neighbors, how "they can't help it." Such compassion from her is new to me; other times, she's her old self and condemns "them" as "crazy."

Eventually, I see that even in the chaos many days are good. Often when I come to visit we sing songs. Sometimes we sing in the corridor, which has chairs and benches along the walls, or in the recreation/dining room. Sitting on a bench, leaning on a walker, a few residents smilingly welcome us and join in, singing "God Bless America," "America the Beautiful," or "Home on the Range." I am proud whenever my mother knows the words. One woman had been a professional singer and still has a beautiful voice. Occasionally, I dance with her as she sings a Spanish love song.

When we sing in my mother's room or the Rose Garden, we choose family favorites: "I've got the sun in the morning and the moon at night," or "Rose-a-Day," which I had performed, seated on the kitchen table when I was about five. My mother especially enjoys "Lolly-Too-Dum," an Appalachian folk song. I usually initiate the singing part of the visit.

One day, my mother sings a Yiddish song about

lovers. I hadn't heard her sing it for a long time, and never at Morningside House.

Lom mir zich iberbaten, iberbaten,
Vos shtestu by die fenster?
Lomir zich iberbaten,
Bist bei mir die shentster.

Lom mir zich iberbaten, iberbaten.
Vos shtestu by dem tir?
Lom mir zich iberbaten, iberbaten
Kum aron tzu mir.

Let us embrace again, embrace my love
Why do you stand by the window.
Let us embrace
You are the prettiest, I know.

Let us embrace my love, embrace again
Why do you stand by the door?
Let us embrace.
Come to me once more.

I see she is happy. The lovers are reconciling. She smiles her own private smile. And doesn't look at me. It dawns on me that the smile is as specific as a color, as a rock -- yet secret. The smile is the one I had seen that day in the car, when she had inadvertently revealed her relationship with Baruch, and disclosed their plan for a hideaway. It is the smile I remembered at my last visit, when I thought back to the time Simon and I had fought over a comic book in dappled sunlight. On this clear day, bits of sun steal through the high branches, leaves flutter, the light trembles; I suddenly realize that it is the smile she makes when she talks about Baruch.

Since now I think I know everything about her, I want to know that secret as well, if only to make certain that her expression, the smile, has meaning, and is not something that happens when she is losing touch. I cannot accept that she is floating; I cannot accept that emptiness -- and that she does not know me.

She sings the song in the Rose Garden. She smiles, I put my arms around her, certain that she is thinking of him,

"So, Momma, you know," I say, "the way you talk about Baruch . . . ," and then I hear myself say what I had never planned to say, what I know will always surprise me with its bluntness, "I think he's my father." This was something I had not permitted myself to dwell on. It was almost fanciful -- a possibility I had pushed away, even as I knew that "the love child" is central in the *Evergreen* story.

I wait for a response. She says nothing.

"So?" I ask.

"So what?" she answers. She is not floating now. She seems assured, in control.

"Soooo. Is he?"

Her smile returns. "I don't know," she finally says. "Isn't that a good answer, 'I don't know'?" And she holds her head high, poised as a ballerina on points.

I think, isn't she something? I am still subordinate to the issue. It remains hers. And I admire her strength as she holds on to her secret. I had dared to ask even more than I had suspected, and she does not deny it. But as much as I applaud her ability to control that information, as much as I respect her tenacity to withhold what she may know, I am determined to learn the truth.

By afternoon, when it is time to go home, so stunned am I by her response -- its elusiveness, its revelation -- that I especially welcome the hour's ride home from Morningside House. I am able to drift, to think and absorb what she had said to me that day.

Usually the changing sky distracts me and helps me decompress from the intensity of being with her: of constantly watching so she does not fall, of listening carefully to make sure I understand each word when she talks to me, and of anticipating her needs -- getting her juice when she is thirsty or making sure she gets to the bathroom in time. But this afternoon, when I think about what I had asked her about Baruch, the sun sets without my knowing. That scene in the Rose Garden follows me home.

What else have I ignored, just allowed to pass by because I did not understand. For most of my life, people had commented on how different I was from my brother and sister -- not only in looks, but in attitude. That was a given. My understanding of our differences was simple: they were children from my parents' good years, when there was money and friends. They had enjoyed the good times. I had supposed that the sudden change in the family's fortune had made my brother and sister more solemn than I was.

My father had owned three bookstores, had traded rare books. I'd heard that he would bring books home for my brother and sister and would tell them Hemingway's 'Nick Adams' stories. My parents had shared dinner with European literati. Those years were lively and happy. My cousin Ann, fifteen years older than I, remarked on those years. "Your mother married your father," she said, "because he was brilliant," adding, "That was what she admired, not his money or his good looks." But I never saw that father. Besides, as a child how could I understand what brilliance was, especially when the Depression had masked him so?

I had seen earlier pictures of my father before the Depression had changed our family's lives. He stood erect; his eyes were clear. He had a full head of hair. I would try to imagine that father. The one I knew was usually hunched over a Hebrew book. Kids coming to our house for the first time would say, "Oh, your grandfather lives with you," and he acted the way grandfathers did then, for first generation children. He barely spoke English, and since school officials had told him not to speak Yiddish to us children, he hardly spoke at all. I would talk for him if we were going anywhere so that his accent would not expose him. He didn't speak to my friends; he just nodded and smiled, not a word, even though he read *The New York*

Times from cover to cover, poring over the paper -- such terrible things were going on in the rest of the world: he was there, with those suffering in the concentration camps.

So he had a language problem and a money problem and a cultural problem and none of them were ever resolved. He carried his Europeanism like a mule, with elegant rare books on his back. The rare books were his real love, often interfering with the business of the store. When times changed, he had to sell many for food. Those he couldn't sell were stored in the basement of the smaller, shabbier apartment building we had moved to. Then the boiler broke. The books were completely destroyed. My father didn't say a word.

In family arguments he'd cough and rant, as though the books' dust from the boiler room had been caught in his throat. Shouting, he'd allude to mythic sources like the Bible or Socrates. By then my mother dismissed his opinions. I remember – vividly -- the Sunday morning he left the classics, and quoted Freud. Depleted by the Depression, his age no longer an advantage, he ranted, "Freud wrote that God kept Moses in the desert for forty years . . . to dispose of old men." That appeal to her, coated in anger, my mother dismissed as self-pity. That he made it at all shocked me, as did her indifference.

So he withdrew to the solace of chess and books. And when he wasn't reading, he was spread out on the sofa, sleeping in his suit, his hair plastered down with gel over his bald spot.

149

Never remembering the good years, not having been dressed in hand-embroidered dresses as my sister had, on my own since my mother went to work, I learned to take care of myself. My Aunt Clara used to call me an urchin. I didn't know about paternal blessings. But there were times when he'd take me rowing in Bronx Park. We'd walk quickly and silently to the bus, as seriously as if we were going to a doctor's appointment. I remember no conversations on those walks, but I do remember thinking how strong he was, as he -- deep in his own thoughts -- rowed the boat, oars splashing water the only sound.

In the car, returning from Morningside, surrounded by the night, I wonder why it matters so: my mother and Baruch have been apart for over half a century. I think of her revealing smile -- now I think, "the Baruch smile."

She seemed pleased even when she found fault with him. As if she were performing, she'd toss her head, and, imitating Baruch, sing-song . . . .

"'I'm in a mood,' he'd say that: 'I'm in a mood.'" She'd laugh out loud! But that would not do. She'd come back to me (Baruch was good for a lesson too): "Rena, don't you give in to a mood." One didn't, like Baruch, submit to a mood. One had to be strong.

She did not need or want a man to lean on. What my mother admired in men surprised me. My mother would sometimes admit that she was attracted to my father's blunt behavior, his disregard for formalities. But not the time her friend came to visit. My father told the friend that my mother wasn't home and shut the door.

No wonder my mother found Baruch's softness appealing. I'd heard many times that when Baruch's daughter admired the moon, he said it was hers, and the river it shimmered in was hers, too, and even a white ocean liner that sailed by, he would tell her, was hers as well.

Baruch, seven thousand miles away, was safe in memories.

Possibly, during the hard times it was Baruch's sweetness that my mother would think back to. Though my sister Bernice often talked about the good times between our parents, I could not imagine them as friends or lovers.

In those years, the air was heavy with cooking and ideas -- but not between my mother and father. He could eat her home-made bread, let her talk, and not say a word. What my father discounted must have beguiled Baruch. He supported her little victories: how she dealt with the janitor or reduced a dinner party to nothing more than dessert.

When she told these stories they always included the Greenbergs' applause: "They laughed when I said, 'Let them fill up at home.'"

I thought she was their darling. Sometimes she'd repeat just the punch-line, "Baruch knew, 'Let them fill up at home.'" But now I understood that there was more between them than two couples "braving the immigrant struggle together," and also that the applause for my mother was often Baruch's alone.

In the night, so tired, my mind wanders as freely as if I am in a deep sleep. I see scenes woven in tapestries, and play parts in fairy tales I'm surprised I remember. I know I cannot simply dream the answers, but that I need evidence as real as the red lights of the car in front of mine. If he were my father . . . I want her to tell me so before she dies. I want her to give me her secret. To give it! That would be my legacy. And I want proof.

Oddly enough I do not have to reach that far back to find it. So much has passed me by that I did not understand.

One morning, only a year or so before, during that time when I had been going to the apartment in Queens a few days a week, my mother and I had been standing in the hallway near the elevator. A neighbor came out of her apartment and asked my mother who I was.

"This is my daughter," she said.

"Really? She doesn't look like you."

"I look like my father," I answered quickly; I knew it was my sister who resembles my mother.

"No, not like Poppa," my mother said.

"Oh, yeah . . . Clara," I said. She was my mother's younger sister. Many family members, even Clara herself, had often said that I looked like her.

"No, like someone long ago," my mother said in an

offhand manner. At the time I didn't think too much about it; I didn't question her because I thought she probably meant her beloved brother Aaron, who had died young, a drowning victim at Coney Island. My mother always cried whenever someone mentioned his name.

I hadn't questioned her at the time, to avoid bringing up a painful memory. Then why does this incident come to me in the car as I drive home tonight after our talk? "Someone long ago." Now it sounds like Baruch.

A Different Mother

XIV

Two Visits

Sitting erect in the car, I am no longer tired; I think of that other car ride, with Shoshana, when she tacitly acknowledged our parents' affair. Earlier that day, during lunch on the deck, Shoshana and my mother had sat together and talked. It was not my mother's nature to dwell on hard times; Shoshana had probably referred to them. I did hear my mother say, "I picked myself up, but not Pinya," referring to my father. Shoshana nodded. Then all of us, Ariel, Ralph, Zach, Laura, and I, joined them at the picnic table. Shoshana told us how her family had come to emigrate to Palestine; how Monya, her mother, had a tantrum, "A tantrum like a child," she said and clenched her fists in the telling -- the stress alive in Shoshana after so many years. At the time, Monya's father had died in Palestine. Because she was not there for his death, Monya insisted that she had to live with family, and they had to move to her sister in Palestine. "My father agreed to go on the condition that mother never complain about the move -- and she never did," Shoshana said, her voice reconciled and proud.

I had not heard Shoshana's version of this story before. On the rare occasions that my mother brought it up, she'd tap her chest and quietly whisper that others held her responsible for their move. I never believed that my mother could have been important enough to get a whole family to move so far away.

Now I think that the move was Monya's scheme to make Baruch leave my mother. The possibility that I had a place in that saga came later that same day, in the car, driving them to New York, when Shoshana made that cryptic reference to Belva Plain's book *Evergreen*.

In the book, a rendezvous with a former lover produces a second child. The protagonist never tells this to her husband, who had inadvertently been responsible for the couple's meeting again. I wonder now whether Shoshana had another reason for recommending the book. Then the inference -- stronger, the message -- that I may also be Baruch's child was too compelling to discuss, probably for Shoshana as well as for me. I had put it aside. It was so long ago, but I had guarded that possibility, gingerly, like eggs in a nest.

Watching Shoshana and my mother together made me think of my meeting with Baruch, one summer, some thirty odd years before, when I had visited with the

Greenberg family in Israel. I sat with Shoshana's father, who was also old, as my mother is now.

The visit to Israel and the Greenberg family had not been planned. I had intended to live in Italy for a year. I was twenty-three years old, and, with money I had saved from my first teaching job and a letter of introduction to a government official from a family friend, I had hoped to get a teaching job there. By the time I got to Italy, the government had fallen once again, and my letter was worthless. Although I did not find a job, I found a letter from Baruch. He wrote, "It is only a short jump over to Israel -- please visit." My mother had probably written to tell the Greenbergs about my adventure. Yes, they were her good friends, but I had no actual memory of them.

I had an uncle in Israel, my mother's other brother, Herschel, who had managed my father's bookstores. After their brother Aaron drowned, he had left for Palestine. Herschel had lived at our house while recovering from an Israeli war injury. I had given him my bicycle to bring back to the kibbutz. My family knew his friends. At the time, I wondered why hadn't my mother written to them rather than to the Greenbergs?

As peculiar as I felt when I received Baruch's letter, I answered and agreed to go. I had consulted no one. At the time an international phone call was out of the question. Even the mail would not be reliable in our family. But the stories my parents told, which were also corroborated by my sister and brother, gave me enough encouragement to accept the invitation.

And, on my very first day, when I saw them standing behind the passenger barrier at the Tel Aviv airport, I knew them. Better, I had the extraordinary sense that I belonged with them: Shoshana's face shone with the familiar smiles of the old photographs, her hands rested on five year old Ilana's shoulders. Ilana's light brown braids were tied with blue ribbons that matched large, blue, attentive eyes. Shoshana's husband, Ariel, held two year old Rachelle in his arms. Monya stood apart, a strong squat seventy-five year old woman, her eyes searching. Baruch could not make it because he was ill. As they stood there, I was pleased at how true they were to the picture I had imagined, and excited by their intense expressions as they looked for me; I had no doubt they were as wonderful as their stories had promised.

At the apartment, Baruch said my trip was daring. I didn't think so. I had prepared and saved for it with less angst than I now plan a dinner party or buy a new dress. Baruch thought it was typical of how my mother brought me up. True, she'd encouraged my going and offered no objections. The only advice she gave the day I left was, "Promise me you'll eat well." And I heard no worry in her voice.

My father, on the other hand, thought it an unnecessary and wasteful extravagance. "It's as if you're putting a match to hundred dollar bills," he said, arranging some old books, behind glass doors, in the foyer bookcase.

"She encourages you to go to the fire," Baruch had said approvingly, referring to the way my mother was bringing me up. On our walks through Jerusalem, Monya would tease me, "She springs like a goat when she walks." And again, "A little goat, Renale . . . you are just like a little goat."

She was warm and welcoming, but not as accepting as Baruch. She was quick to point out that my dress was dirty around the neck and not up to my mother's standards of cleanliness and spiffiness.

"No, Chana would never wear the dress that way," she said. I was somewhat surprised that her only comment about my mother would be so quotidian. But then, my mother often made snide comments regarding Monya's domestic inadequacies, her dalliances, and Monya's snobbery about being a professional. Monya noticed collars, but I knew, from stories, how superior my mother felt. She'd brag about how much Baruch loved the cozy commotion in our home.

At any rate, their opinions didn't bother me. I lived with Shoshana and Ariel and had fun with their adorable daughters, a marvelous balance to the serious adults. In the afternoons, after working at her job as an editor, Shoshana took me on errands with the children. Sometimes, we would visit Baruch and Monya, who lived nearby. Shoshana fussed over me. I was the first baby she had felt an adult to, and she often said that I was the hardest part of America to leave.

159

My family had put up people from "other times," and
so I was totally at ease being that person from "other
times" to Shoshana's children. I felt no barriers. I was
open and happy and welcomed this as a way to see the
world.

For all his enthusiasm, Baruch was ill, recovering
from an operation. I saw him only as an old sick man.
Once, Monya asked me to stay with him while she did her
errands.

I sat next to his bed and we talked. He told me a
curious story about how my cousin on the kibbutz came to
understand death as a child (saving a butterfly in a
matchbox, only to discover it dead the following day).
Baruch asked me -- tested me -- about Herzl, the father of
Zionism; I found it odd to be talking history. Though he lay
on the bed, I had the surreal impression we were in a
classroom, actually, a lecture hall. Next to the dresser,
with hairbrushes on its lace doily, bookcases overflowed
with English and Hebrew books -- perfect props for
Baruch's professorial pose. The books, shoved helter-
skelter, papers sticking out, portrayed a busy life, no less
than the lines etched in his thin, pale aging face revealed
his present fragility. I may have given the information
that I once belonged to a Zionist Youth organization, but I
wasn't sure whether he was listening. I thought he was
tired; maybe he needed to sleep. I looked at the disheveled
pillows, revealing a long time in bed, blankets and sheets
askew, and waited.

"So Renale, tell me about momma, poppa?" he finally asked.

He was surprised to learn that they voted, that my father was a citizen. "So, he votes? He is a citizen?" And then Baruch said something about amnesty for illegal immigrants after World War I.

Oh, so that's why they left America, I remember thinking. He seemed more outgoing than my father. Was it because Baruch wasn't hiding anything? I looked at him, another old man in bed. He seemed to be wondering about this amnesty question. I felt him debating his decision to leave America. Amnesty. Who knew what else tormented him. I felt sorry for my parents' generation.

"So tell me," he said. "How is it in your house? Tell me, for example, a day."

I wonder, now, if he framed his question to avoid asking specifically about my mother. Oblivious to a possible scheme or veiled motive, I eagerly described our Sunday mornings at home: how I would wake up often to find my mother washing the kitchen window and how pleased and enthusiastic she would be.

"See," she would confide to me as if she had stolen the time, "While you slept, I did it all, and the window thanks me." Our fifth-floor apartment had a view of the sky -- a luxury compared to most apartments that looked out on brick masonry. Our family often talked about the beauty of the changing sky, and the sun pouring in. I was sure to make this point to Baruch. I was proud of her

Sunday morning celebrations and I was careful to quote
her accurately.

"After all, everyone is sleeping," she would whisper,
defending her assault on the kitchen, "and this way . . . ,"
and she'd justify her weekly cleaning that included
washing the walls. I told him how the aroma of onions and
mushrooms simmering on the stove welcomed me. There
would be fresh bagels or rye bread to eat them on.

"Mushrooms and onions," he repeated with a sick
man's smile -- half memory, half desire.

I described my mother's rooster collection, hung like
pictures on the wall. Sitting at the kitchen table, we'd see
roosters of different sizes, made with different materials:
straw, wrought iron, one of Delft blue-and-white porcelain
-- even one made of cardboard rated a place because it had
"personality."

"Look at his comb," I imitated how she described a
stylized rooster with a yellow comb askew. "He looks like
he's had a fight with the hens. You know, usually there's
only one rooster," she explained; "the hens lay the eggs
after all. See, this one looks like he's crowing. See how he
holds his head, "cock-a-doodle-doo," and she'd cock her head
pertly to the side, which I did to show Baruch, and then
told him how she'd crow -- as loud as any rooster she left in
her small town in Russia, no longer concerned for the
others asleep.

He laughed as I told him my stories, and then
speaking softly, faintly -- after all, he was ill -- he asked,

"Do they sleep in the same bed now?"

I felt as if he had shouted. My parents' relationship was something I had learned to live with: my father's excessive sleeping, my mother's manic energy, and -- then unexplainable to me -- a crazy unspoken regard they seemed to have for each other, but at other times a total disregard, long periods of not talking. My parents' marriage -- after years of sleeping in separate rooms, they once again shared a bedroom -- was family business I did not report on. I had learned not to allow it be a major concern of mine.

I must have turned away, when -- a truck may have backfired, or a draft blew the curtains -- a disturbance brought me back. I saw Baruch staring at the ceiling, and then I heard him, an old sick rooster, say, ". . . and he left her unsatisfied." That is all I remember. I left my post by the side of his bed.

I was shocked that he would violate her privacy -- mine as well. My mother baked pies, she washed windows, she told stories, she crowed. Who was he to talk about my mother's sex life to me? How could he? Would he have asked that of my sister?

The scene remains vivid after thirty-five years, when Shoshana brings up *Evergreen* on the ride back. But at the time the possibility that Baruch and my mother could have had an affair still did not occur to me.

After spending time with the Greenbergs, I visited my uncle's family on the kibbutz. My cousin laughed at the butterfly story. I spent time with Monya's sister in Tel Aviv. I traveled on buses to other cities. I saw Senhedrin, a court of justice that was five thousand years old. I went to Athens, the Acropolis, Paris, and Montmarte: thrilling sights to a young girl. Then home. Now, I confuse memories of the Acropolis with pictures in books. But it is that scene with Baruch in Jerusalem that I am unable to forget.

All her life my mother had flaunted her sexuality, but only in her old age would I truly understand the extent of it. Even in my childhood her *joie de vivre* was legendary. Sunsets and starry nights, folk songs and opera, Van Gogh and Gauguin, and bawdy jokes: she owned them all. I knew that. Vital, vibrant, unconventional -- I did not translate that energy (often hostile and aggressive as well) into sexuality.

Not that she ever hid her delight. In fact, she told me my first dirty joke and waited for one from me. Years later, she explained that what she wanted was that I share what I learned on the streets. She didn't want me to be afraid of sex. Our house was casual about sex as well.

I remember my sister and me floating around the apartment naked, like the dancers in a Matisse painting. About the triangle of hair that had started to appear, my mother would greet it with her carefree proclamation: "Here she comes with Trotsky's beard." When either of us wandered into a room for a book or an apple, "Here she comes with Trotsky's beard," she'd almost sing, and so take on her attitude towards both sex and the Bolshevik cause. She was not timid.

At times she would glance at my developing breasts approvingly and tell me about restaurants in Paris where waitresses worked bare to the waist. Her telling had no sleazy "topless bar" innuendo, nor any of the wonder or enthusiasm for the blooming anemone. She'd make these comments with the same assurance she had when she decided which color gloves would go with an outfit, or when she knew there was just the right amount of pepper in the soup. "Yes, they would take you," she'd say with that sureness about me working half-naked in a Parisian cafe.

We never admitted that there was anything sensual or erotic about our nudity. "Your skin has to breathe," we'd say. We three Trefman women at that time all slept naked, no pillow either, just ourselves, "our bodies" (we'd caringly reflect) in our beds with a duvet covered quilt, European style.

During those times, my brother and father fade. We women didn't worry about them. They were not part of the parade, they never stopped what they were doing because of us; they made no comments.

Sex was like breathing, my mother used to say, but to be treasured, like air after a rain; no one would choose to breathe in a sewer. Still, at the time, her talk appeared to be mostly theory.

*   *   *

Now, as I drive down the dark highway, the scenes

flash by like so many traffic signs. I see us talking on walks, or shopping; I remember thinking how fascinated my mother was by Monya's audacity, and by the daring twenties. What madness! What had escaped me was that my flamboyant mother, usually so open, could have been involved in an intrigue of her own. And those stories she told about Monya -- her abortions, her dalliances -- as if she, my mother, were virtue personified. I forgot that my mother lived in the daring twenties as well. Now I believe she was justifying what she and Baruch were doing. With all the sexual candidness in our house, at the time I thought of my mother as free, uninhibited, but not actually sexual. When my parents shared their bedroom, with its ornate furniture, I did not imagine that anything went on in it. Even as a married woman I had remained their young daughter. Looking back, I realized she had always kept that part of her life to herself. Her resistance in the Rose Garden earlier held the kernel of her secret private pleasure.

XV

A NEW MOTHER

The moon's light bending into my car reminds me of where I am. In the left corner of the windshield I see the big yellow disk, leading me down the highway. Finally I am aware of small towns, the few buildings that appear between gas stations and diners. As I drive in the quiet night, my mother's enigma goes round and round in my head, like the tires rolling me home. My children are older than I had been on that visit to Israel, yet I am still in the dark, giddy, tired, with unexpected memories shooting out of the night.

I had married a year after my trip to Israel and Europe. A year later, my mother left my father. Because I took my mother's side in the breakup, we never spoke again.

My young children kept me busy, too busy to keep up with my mother's difficult life. Not that I could make up

for her factory problems, her faulty sewing machine, or the
fact that work wasn't divided fairly during the "slow
season." She went for a practical nursing license and then
took a beautician's course. But her problems with them,
their "challenges," no longer interested me. She said
keeping her fingers occupied relieved anxiety and put extra
money in her hands. But what I think she found most
rewarding was the high ground she could take when she
criticized how I took care of the children or how I wore my
hair.

Not only was there nothing I could do about her
problems, she wouldn't listen to any of my suggestions. I
didn't want her advice either. She was out of touch with
the conformity I embraced, a relief from the chaotic
household of my childhood. She, of course would say
almost anything (to my family and, worse, to my new
friends) and not worry about the consequences.

During the hard time between Ralph and me, she'd
tell me that a married woman could go to a dance -- with an
escort, a man other than her husband. Sometimes, *à la*
Madame Bovary or Anna Karenina, it didn't work out . . . .
But, she assured me, such things were done: "That was the
European way."

This sophistication was not for me. For her,
infidelity could be a joke. She liked the one about a boy
who goes to his father to tell him that he is in love and
wants to marry Mary, a neighborhood girl. "You can't
marry Mary," the father says, "She's your sister." The boy,

very distraught, tells his mother what his father said. "Marry her," the mother says, "He's not your father."

I guess I just wasn't listening carefully enough to what she was really saying.

During those early years, there were many times she'd kept me waiting at the bus stop when she was expected for a visit. My car filled with groceries, I'd be on tenterhooks, knowing the children were alone for too long. Waiting, I'd worry that she had had a heart attack or an accident, only to learn that she had missed the bus agreed upon because she had impulsively decided to bring some delicacy like a tongue or farmer cheese for blintzes -- items not available in my town -- or because she'd met someone she hadn't seen in a long time. Relieved that nothing terrible had happened, I'd forgive her. Other times, when I had fun and she was not there, I'd feel guilty.

During this period she usually looked vibrant, her hair stylishly coifed and dyed a youthful black. She wore the latest New York styles, always at least a season ahead of me. She talked about the trips she took and people she met on the bus to Niagara Falls or to Pennsylvania. I admired her resourcefulness and, despite all our differences, ached because she did not have a partner, a boyfriend or even another husband like many of my friends' mothers had acquired.

As it turned out, she did. Years later -- when my children were in college -- my mother told me, so lightly, not pausing as she opened and closed her refrigerator door, that for almost twelve years she had had a lover.

"There was someone," she said, and then casually, as if she were reminding me to take an umbrella on a rainy day, added, "but now it's over. I sent him away."

I was seated on her golden couch. The water was running at the sink. Maybe she thought I hadn't heard, but I couldn't speak. She turned away and rinsed a dish. When I was able, I asked why she hadn't told me. She answered matter-of-factly, "I always thought it would end."

Timidly I asked, "Are you sure it's over now?"

"I sent him away," she said, "and I did it so he won't come back." She seemed as proud as if she'd scrubbed a tough stain out of a favorite dress.

I was too stunned to ask why, but after a rare silence between us she went on, "He asked me to marry him, so I sent him away." She had her reasons.

"He had a sick wife. She was in a nursing home. When she died he asked me to marry him," she said.

She acted as if that were the end of the story. My throat was so dry I could only manage a weak, "So why didn't you?" I felt ridiculous prodding her, but it was easier than asking her again why she hadn't told me, why she had led me to believe she led a different life.

"What, marry a man who cheats on his wife? He'd cheat on me the first chance too!"

I felt as though I'd been brought up in a convent, so removed was I from this freewheeling independence. Knocked overboard, I floated for a while, grasping at the

notion that for twelve years her private life had flourished
while I had agonized about its bleakness. And she had
ended it so abruptly: *Finí!* It was as if she had pressed a
button: there'd been no time for me to feel happy for her. I
felt cheated for all the worry and sympathy I had
expended. The sexual affair itself was not the issue for me:
after all, she was a widow. Besides, it was the seventies,
and the sexual revolution was in full swing. I could
understand her wanting a man, but why didn't she tell me.
That's what upset me the most.

Now as I drive home from Morningside House with
my new discovery about Baruch, I do not feel cheated or
upset at all: "I am here and she remembers him with love,"
is my only thought.

I have been a child so long. I realize I had spent
energy on the wrong emotions. I had been sorry for my
mother, but she had taken care of herself. Back then,
when she had told me about her lover, because of my anger
at her, I had not seen how she valued her independence.
This time, her secrecy about Baruch delights me. I
understand that she cherishes her secret.

Once home I feel breathless. So good to be home, to
see Ralph working at the dining room table. I am not
ready to talk to him about the matter again. We had not
discussed it since Shoshana's visit, the first time I realized
that my mother could have had an affair. "It's possible,"
we had agreed. Then let it be.

This time I want to keep my mother's secret awhile.

I have a new mother to think about as well. The evening passes with both of us involved with our own thoughts, and before I know it, I am in bed, at ease with the drone of Ralph's snoring. At ease, but still too stimulated to sleep. I am remembering. I must have been about ten, in bed, not yet asleep, and heard my parents talking through the bedroom wall, when suddenly I realized they were talking about me.

"No," I heard my mother say, "She is not going to Hebrew school. The others went, and what do they remember? Nothing!" My father muttered something in reply.

But my mother, loud -- the dark did not soften her voice -- insisted, "She is not going. She will learn Yiddish. She is mine." I was thrilled. I never imagined that I was a topic worthy of discussion; concern was usually for my older, somehow more important, brother and sister. I remember thinking "she is mine" meant "my project," because, in this instance, Simon and Bernice had not only forgotten their Hebrew, but had also stopped speaking Yiddish.

I became hopeful: possibly my mother's "she is mine" meant "she is my favorite," which with her making a living -- the washing and shopping and cooking -- was not something any of us could feel sure of. True, we were acknowledged: Bernice so beautiful, so brilliant; Simon, profound, philosophical. I, the youngest, was left with personality and spunk. We all felt we lacked the attributes of the others; none of us could be the favorite.

In bed, an adult, I smile, realizing I had not been bold enough; I had played with daring possibilities -- that my education was of major concern, that I -- who was not brilliant or profound -- might be the favorite. . . . But one possibility was beyond my understanding. In bed with a husband of my own sleeping beside me, I reach beyond my ten year old's knowledge. I hear the words again: "She is mine." Then I consider that in saying "She is mine," she had meant "She is not yours."

A Different Mother

XVI

Jacoby City Hospital

My mother is in the hospital again, the second time
in the three months she's been in Morningside House.
After her first ten days at there, just before Thanksgiving,
she was admitted to Jacoby Hospital because of congestive
heart failure. At that time, I was not upset about the
diagnosis, since that had happened often when she lived
alone. She would call 911 in the middle of the night. I'd
get a call from the hospital to the effect that as soon as the
excess fluids that had accumulated in her lungs had been
drained she would be discharged. But this time I was
afraid because of the Medicare constraints: her first thirty
days in a nursing home have to be consecutive; she might
lose her place at Morningside House.

At that first visit, she had been admitted to the
hospital on a Thursday, and on the following day I was told
she was fine. Her discharge was held up because the

doctor could not be found to sign the necessary forms. On Saturday the resident was satisfied that she could be discharged, but transportation to her nursing home was not available. I told him I'd be happy to drive her there. However, then there were a series of communication mishaps with Morningside House -- messages not received. When I got to Morningside House with my mother in the car, I discovered that readmitting her on a Saturday presented problems.

Actually, there had been no reason to be in such a rush. The doctors and aides at Jacoby were friendly to her. She did not appear neglected, except that they would not allow her to go to the bathroom. She might fall, they said. Nor would they allow me the responsibility of handling the bedpan. I hadn't realized this would make her incontinent.

Morningside House had been so wonderful: I was quite embarrassed at having pushed my mother through, causing complications in the re-admission process. An important certification was missing: the PRI. The hospital had not provided the forms verifying her status, which could have changed in the course of her hospitalization.

It was fall, when the air was crisp and the sun still high. Earl Collum, her social worker at Morningside, was brisk and efficient. He relieved my anxiety, and we put the experience behind us.

In retrospect I think of how in synch the weather had been with the experience -- a tidy metaphor for what had happened. Now, when my mother has to be admitted to the hospital again, the sense of that brisk efficiency associated with autumn is missing. Somehow the cold, gray iciness of this last week in December permeates the hospital. My mother's bed is in the last room at the end of the hall, indicative of the end-of-the-line care I am afraid she may receive. Yet, after that experience of her first hospital admission from Morningside House and my pushing her through and causing so much administrative work for them, I restrained myself, but remained alert to bureaucratic sabotage like excessive forms and transportation on weekends.

To protect her, I inform the doctor that my mother is not to receive aggressive treatment: we only want her to be made comfortable; she is 89, frail and disoriented, and suffers from serious heart disease. Her doctors at Morningside House, myself, and my mother have all agreed on this.

At Morningside House, the doctor had come up to my mother's floor one day when I was there. He sat down at a folding table in the living room. "Mrs. Trefman, we would like to know what your feelings are about your treatment if you should get sick," he said.

My mother nodded, acknowledging his question. He waited for her to think it through.

"If your heart stops beating, or has trouble, what would you like us to do?" he asked, and waited again.

My mother said, "Try a little, and if nothing happens, leave it. You know, doctor, we all die, we all die

177

sometime. So try a little and then let it be what will be," and she signed the form.

Tuesday morning at Jacoby Hospital, Dr. Brownstein, a resident, appears warm and attentive to her. He assures me that his examination indicates that she will be leaving by the end of the week.

On my visit the following day, I learn that my mother has climbed out of bed, pulled out her catheter and her IV. So I am able to accept that she is restrained with a Posey. This is preferable to wrist restraints, because her hands are free to scratch an itch, blow her nose, or hold a glass of water. She is alert and greets me cheerfully. Dr. Brownstein, who is joking with her, again tells me that she will be discharged by the end of the week.

I intend to visit her every day when she is in the hospital, since I know how difficult a strange place is for her. Unfortunately, I have car trouble on Thursday and cannot make it. On the phone I learn that she is getting a cardiac echo test. Although I know that the procedure is not invasive, I am afraid this will be the beginning of a series of tests or that her condition has worsened. Dr. Travis, the attending physician, assures me the tests gauge her condition so that her medicines can be adjusted to make her more comfortable. Everything sounds considerate and humane. But little do I realize that is the last time I will feel that way about Jacoby.

To avoid the problems of her last discharge, I call the hospital at 7:30 on Friday morning, and ask them to start the necessary paperwork. The person answers perfunctorily, saying she is busy working on charts, but will give the message to the unit nurse.

Visiting hours start at 2:30 p.m. and I enter the hospital with the feeling that I have already accomplished something for my mother. I have set her discharge in motion. The elevator doors open and I take long confident steps down the corridor to her room. However, once I open the door I realize my confidence has been based on an illusion. My mother is naked except for a diaper, tied to a chair, feces oozing out the back of her diaper. I look for the nurse or nurse's aide. I assume they have been working on her, but no one is near by. Finally, more as a question than a statement, I say, "My mother is naked." I cannot believe that on this December day her being naked is not part of an examination.

"We have no nightgowns," an aide says, and walks away. A strange thing happens to the relatives of the elderly in these situations. We see something is wrong -- and become afraid to believe what we see or to voice our objections. We know they can take it out on the patient when we are not there, especially if this happens during visiting hours. The aide walks away, and I sheepishly, because I have no authority, almost surreptitiously, as if I am trapped or performing an underground act, wrap my mother in my winter jacket, holding back my anger at the aide for what she has done and at myself for taking it.

As I wrap my mother in my winter jacket, the

women in the next bed wakes up and points to her nightgown on the third, empty, bed. "It's there; she took it off." I dress my mother, and at my request an aide changes her. Unfortunately, my mother defecates again. I apologize and tell the aide that she needs another change.

"I changed her," she says and then adds, "I have other patients. Besides, there are no diapers." Eventually she finds some linen to wrap around her. Since my mother is to be discharged, I want to walk her, both to maintain her stamina, and more important, to make sure, that she doesn't "forget" how to walk -- a problem with Alzheimer's disease. She had been admitted on a 911, and so does not have her robe or slippers with her. I ask if these could be provided.

"We have none," is the answer.

I beg and receive a pair of slippers in an adjacent corridor, take her for a short walk and put her back to bed. It is now 3 p.m. I finally find Dr. Travis, who says she can leave that afternoon, or Saturday. The doctor is not apologetic as she regards my experience that afternoon. "This is a different world," she says, about the hospital. "You were both right. Of course, your mother needs to be walked: She could lose it." She means my mother could forget how to walk. "But you will have to walk her," she adds. That part is fine with me. We were "both right," she says, but I am in the hospital now, where that world rules.

When I ask if the paper work was done, I am referred to the social worker, Mr. Ibrahim. He tells me not

180

to worry about her getting out, or losing her place at
Morningside House, that she can stay at Jacoby for twenty-
one days. However, both Dr. Travis and I urge him to
check the procedure for discharging her the following day
or that afternoon. He says that since it is 3 p.m. it is too
late to start a PRI, which is the status report necessary
before she can be readmitted to Morningside House. They
need to know if she will be able to function at her pre-
hospitalization level. Filling out a PRI does not entail long
or complicated examinations: it is simply a checklist that, I
will learn -- but do not know at this time -- usually takes
fifteen minutes. Maybe there was a hospital party that
afternoon.

"Sorry, but you are caught up in the bureaucracy,"
he says. My mother will have to stay till Tuesday, since it
is the New Year's Day weekend.

Still sensitive to complications I'd caused
Morningside House when I forced her discharge the last
time, I decide not to insist on her discharge now. Possibly
she may benefit from the hospital care. What has
happened today was an aberration, I tell myself; it will not
happen again. Her first visit to Jacoby was not like this,
and I decide to relax.

So the next day, although the roads are treacherous,
Ralph and I get to the hospital by 2 p.m. Again we wrap a
sheet over her nightgown and take her for a long walk -- as
far as the dental clinic and back. She is not sure who
Ralph is, seems surprised to hear we are married, even

more so that his family has accepted me.

Sunday, and the roads are icy; after my car spins around on the ice, I decide not to visit. I call, explain I cannot be there, and ask if it would be possible to help her with just a few steps after a diaper change. "I live in New Jersey, too," the nurse says, "Our other patients are in life threatening situations." I understand that my mother is their lowest priority and is there only because they had not bothered to do the paper work. Yet I know by now that her senility is as much a disease as her weak heart: Care, which may not require sophisticated equipment, is crucial. Loss of function, such as the ability to walk, escalates quickly and is often permanent. Ironically, each loss costs society more and is painful for the individual as well. Once a patient can't walk, she has to be lifted; bed sores may develop and become difficult to cure; dressings and medications have to be applied. A person may have to feed her if she is not encouraged to feed herself. Diapers have to be changed and supplied if she is encouraged to become incontinent. Despair escalates as well. I see that in our crazy economy we are all paying.

On New Year's Day, Laura and I find my mother restrained by her wrists, howling in a torn wet diaper. We release her, dress her in the robe I have brought, and take her for a short walk. She tires quickly. When she asks for a drink, the aide says, "This is a holiday; there are no clean cups."

Laura stays with my mother while I walk down the

hall, wash out a cup near her bed that had phlegm in it. Then my daughter and I change her diaper. We want to leave her unrestrained. The nurse had said that the doctor had prescribed wrist restraints, but once we tell her that we have a Posey she agrees to it.

The next day the holiday is over, and on January 2nd my mother is finally discharged.

A Different Mother

XVII

Back to Morningside

"See if she'll eat that. We want to fatten her up," Carrie, her aide, says. Angela greets us, "Anna, tastes good?" she asks my mother and hugs us both.

We are back at Morningside House. Carrie feeds her slowly, walks her, and listens to her. After a few days my mother is able to use the toilet.

I am glad to be at Morningside as well. I am ready to wheel my mother down to the library for a change of place, but Carrie stops me and runs to the pantry for another Ensure pudding, a therapeutic high calorie nutrient enrichment. "See if you can get her to eat a little of it when you're downstairs," she says, smiling.

I meet with the Vice President and the doctor, who is Chief of Medicine. Their eyes tear when I tell them what has happened during her stay at Jacoby. I beg them to let her die before calling Jacoby again. The doctor offers to take my mother on his private service at Einstein or Montefiore Hospitals.

When I call Jacoby to complain, Carol Millet, then in charge, makes no excuses, only repeats, as if it were policy, what Dr. Travis had said: "This is a city hospital; what do you expect?" The irony, of course, is that my mother was kept at Jacoby three days longer than necessary, at a probable cost to society of $6,000. How cynical that their "professional" behavior and waste creates such a gulag.

"You are both right," Dr. Travis had confided to me. As if she were teaching me a great truth -- something like "always cross at the green" or "chew your food." "You are both right," she had said, as if she were being fair.

It is spring and my mother has amazingly gained weight. She walks, and talks. We all feel so lucky that we have found such a wonderful nursing home. In fact, my husband says that if his life ever came to this, he would want to come to the same facility. When I tell this to my friends, they cringe.

"Well, would you want your kids to have all the responsibility?" I ask them.

"No, kill me," one says. But I know how special the staff is, how much they care for the residents, how complaints and joys are validated, agitation acknowledged, assurance given, not drugs. A quandary about which color lipstick to choose is not dismissed: hair is combed, men are shaved, a tie is thoughtfully chosen.

Along with my mother's decline, something new transcends her frailty, her toothlessness, and her requests to visit her dead mother, dead sisters, and her questions about my "babies," who are now adult children. After years of being partial to my sons, she finally makes up to my daughter. Each time we visit, she apologizes to Laura and to me -- separately.

"I was not good to you in your troubles," she says to her when they are alone. She refers to the period when Laura had taken time off from college, and to her other difficulties along the way.

"I never knew she would work out so well, so understanding -- more so than you," she confides to me when we are alone, adding that familiar jab, just to prove she has not gone completely soft. Obliquely, she will say that the people are good to her. One afternoon, resting in her spotless sunny room, she calls to me. "You know, " she whispers, "we must leave."

She misses her home, her other life, I think, and say, "When you are stronger, I will take you home."

"No, now," she answers. What is her sudden urgency? "They will tire of me here. How long can they keep this up? Let's leave before they throw me out." My mother's *modus operandi* was always combative. She goes on the offensive so as not to have to be on the defensive. If a person was "good enough" to be her friend, she would assume that person would probably not want to be a friend. Often she'd bully someone she thought had the ability to

187

improve. She'd taught English to Spanish and Russian immigrants she'd met at the bakery, given a dashing hairdo to a shy girl in her apartment building; once she encouraged a busboy to become a waiter. "After all," she explained, "a waiter is already a small business man; you can make money."

My mother has never been cared for. She didn't allow it. She was too independent. Suddenly she can no longer care for herself, barely walking, except at night, when she wanders uncontrollably, a symptom of her senility. When she was able to go to SHARE, a special day program, I asked her if she was happy to see Michael, the director of the program.

"Happy to see him? Happy to see Michael?" she asked, her eyes glowing and a toothless grin taking over her thin face, "You could never know how great he is, how great the people here are; they treat me as if I'm not sick. I never knew people could be so good."

My mother always had to be strong, and would never submit to despair, though my brother's death, her one acknowledged tragedy, was enough of an excuse for that. The winter after he died, she decided to spend a few months in California in order "... to be among strangers. Then if someone says 'good morning,' I will have to answer with a smile."

Now she's saying so much I had never expected to hear, almost a complete turn-around from her usual attitudes. She never wanted to teach me Russian, either.

It was the language she and my father spoke when they did not want the children to understand. I used to ask her to teach it to me, probably to learn their secrets, but she wouldn't.

"You will only break your teeth on it, and besides how can I teach the language of anti-Semites." Yet, years before *Glasnost*, she always quoted the proverbs, the poetry, the literature, and later taught Russian to Zach, who became fluent in it.

"You must be able to converse with the enemy. He can do that," she explained when I asked her why she taught Zach and not me. But I had sensed that her bitterness had softened. Later, when she had begun to fail, just before she moved to Morningside House, she said she wanted to teach me Russian, but by then I wasn't willing.

Now on these pleasant spring days we go down to the Rose Garden and admire the sky and flowers. We talk. She tells me I am pretty. I take up her offer to finally teach me Russian -- a souvenir of this time together.

At each visit, I learn a word or two. This takes place anywhere, in the corridors, her room, the Rose Garden at Morningside House, or next to her bed in the hospital, whenever I want her to be in charge.

She reviews my vocabulary and corrects my pronunciation. She is very demanding, very exacting and particular about the pronunciation – *blyu* might come out sounding like *blya* or *blyiu.* I yield to her judgement, trusting her demands completely as I struggle to pronounce

189

the sound exactly right. When I finally say it to her satisfaction, she nods, tells me to say it again, refines it, corrects it again, drills me -- heaven.

I learn to say, "I want," and make up phrases, adding "a book," "work," and without planning, find myself murmuring, "*Chatchu*," I want, "*moiya mammuh*."

XVIII

New Club / Picnic Interrupted

My mother is always on my mind, and I recognize women I barely know going through the same stage of life: worry for a sick aging parent -- not able to let go.

On the checkout line in the supermarket these same women, who were always well groomed, are now disheveled, their usual reserve usurped as their stories flood out. Before, on chance meetings, we'd talk about our children's landmarks or our own -- a vacation, an achievement, even an operation. Now each one earnestly tells me how consumed she is with her mother's care. Not really friends, we become intimate: their confidence shaken, they cannot believe that they are witnessing this. It is frightening, wearing, to see your mother lose her abilities, more remarkable than watching babies learn new skills. It starts slowly, so slow that it's merely an irritation. I can hear it happening as these women talk.

"I know she can't help it, I understand," a friend says about her mother. "And I am understanding for awhile. But there is a limit to my understanding." My friend still feels free enough to complain. Soon she will have to balance their old relationship -- as important as her mother's physical condition -- with her supervision of the medications (does she take the pills as prescribed?) and doctor visits (never mind finding one who cares).

The same friend complains that her mother doesn't seem to hear her when she speaks to her.

"Get her a hearing aid. Insist on it, so that she gets all the help possible," I say, daring to speak with authority, conviction.

"I could never do that," my friend says.

I should know she can't tell her mother what to do. If I try to tell mine, my mother's voice, real and imagined, reproaches me, "Rena, you know better than to tell me what to do."

That has always been the case, and does not change even as her condition worsens at Morningside House. When an aide is ready to escort my mother to the beauty parlor and she refuses, he says, "Mrs. Trefman, your daughter says you should get a haircut."

My mother quickly corrects him. "She is still only the daughter, and the daughter doesn't tell the mother what to do. I am the mother." She does not go to the beauty parlor.

No one could tell my mother what to do. When we were growing up, there was a short time that she and my

sister's friend's mother were friendly. The woman, a
communist, tried to recruit my mother into the party. "And
if I don't want strawberries and cream," my mother argued,
"no one tells me how to live." This woman had been a
dentist, had been divorced, and at the time was a social
worker. It was clear she could do anything. But if she
thought she could dictate to my mother, she learned
otherwise. Talking about their lives, they'd argue whether
children should know the family's financial situation, or
other parental concerns. My mother had no doubts: "No,
children should know that there's food on the table and a
warm bed to sleep in; that's what they should know," she
would say. So, when I hear that tone, that surety feels as
good as a lullaby. I am glad whenever she has the last
word.

My friend will need time before she understands how
these annoyances will become tragedy.

"And then this doctor didn't listen. He put her in the
hospital and didn't check her urine even though she
complained about burning. Well, we learned she had a
high grade fever and a cracked pelvic bone."

Whenever a doctor tried dismissing my mother's
complaints, telling her that she had to learn to live with it
because she was old, my mother would bellow, "Time for
another doctor." The new doctor might look at her with a
fresh perspective, or might be more thorough, or something
new might have developed to the point where it was
recognizable and treatable: my mother would be more

comfortable and the doctor would be a hero in her eyes. My mother deserved credit for her perseverance. I know she took care of herself; she took care of her health, her clothes and, yes, took care of herself in ways I had not considered.

She tested her doctors, questioning her medicines, and even with the correct medicines there were always side-effects. Sometimes the pills did damage: once, while she lived in her apartment, a diuretic washed out her potassium; she could hardly speak, her memory was spotty, she walked with difficulty. The side-effect may not be medical: a diuretic makes the face look pinched, robbing it of fluid, thus distorting expressions that show emotions -- sadness becomes tragic, and a smile is suddenly sharp. My mother began to look like a bird.

My friend, exasperated, adds, "And when we put her in the hospital . . . ."

"Oh," I am now the voice of experience: "Old people can't take the hospital. They become psychotic."

She wants to tell me everything. "She was off the wall," she murmurs, "off the wall."

The most a doctor said to prepare me when my mother went to the hospital for gastro-enteritis, a few years earlier, was that "old people can't take the hospital." I didn't know old minds and did not expect her vacant stare and bizarre questions, either, while she was there.

My friends don't talk about the other problems -- the anger, the shift in family dynamics, how a parent courts the negligent child (now sixty or seventy years old), and how old arguments surface; they only wonder what to do.

I used to think more women than men were in nursing homes because women are usually younger than their husbands and care for them at home. Or that because men died younger they escaped the scourge of Alzheimer's. I've since learned that women are more likely to become afflicted with Alzheimer's. As I listen to the "mother stories" so earnestly confided to me in the supermarket, I realize we share a milestone after all. We have grown up. I guess when you have to parent your parents you are finally all grown up.

So I am grateful that my mother is in Morningside House. The staff helps me as well. I trust them. But I cannot let go; I do not plan parties or vacations for myself.

"Plan, you can always cancel," Ralph's younger cousin advises me. Then, one Sunday in August, I have a barbecue for Ralph's cousins who have recently emigrated from Russia. Just as the food is ready -- tuna off the grill, fresh corn steaming--the phone rings. It is Morningside House, informing me that that my mother is being admitted to the hospital -- Jacoby. They are the only ones who have an emergency room.

"No, don't send her to the hospital, not there -- I've written it down . . . ." I suppress a scream into the phone. Six-year-old Ilya is racing in and out; the house is full of company arguing intensely about world events.

"You don't know me, I'm from the night shift," the

voice on the phone says, trying to reassure me. "I love your mother, her stories about her father, about her childhood in Russia," and then in a low voice, "I understand death with dignity, but she's in pain."

Soon women are in the kitchen cleaning; a cousin stacks the dishwasher her way -- correcting my slap-dash system. Now, whenever I place a serving spoon in its proper compartment, it will bring back the interrupted picnic, the delay at the bridge, my mother's frightened face, and her relieved smile when she sees me in the emergency room. I remain until I am certain that she will be transferred to Montefiore Hospital, as the nurse at Morningside has promised to arrange. There, unlike at Jacoby, I find kindness and professional awareness prevail; there are specific protocols to accommodate her senility -- she is placed on the toilet and walked. Also, for a few hours each day, she is seated near the nurses' station, where they dispense a friendly word to her on their way to other patients. Her frailty is regarded tenderly.

Now back at Morningside House, I see that my mother often looks like a skeleton. She can barely breathe. But her eyes shine with life, even now. So I can smile and think of her brightness -- and of her secret happiness.

An aide at the nursing home tells me there are many times when she leaves for the day certain that my mother will die during the night. The aide says that when she returns the next morning she learns that a healthy person on the floor has died.

I know that my mother has told the angel of death to go next door, to leave her alone. She is not ready.

Someone questions the time I spend with my mother. I am not sure whether I am looking for life in her or death. I stay with my mother to see if she is well, or well-treated, or, not trusting her new demeanor -- she has become soft -- waiting for a glimpse of the old fight in her. I stay, I cannot let go, I wait. I want to see her, knowing she is at the cusp of her existence.

One winter day as the janitor mops the floor in my mother's room. I say, "It's really hot in here," I say it as much to complain as to talk to him.

"It has to be; these people are old. Old people need to be warm. They're not like us," he says, "They can't take the cold." Although there is a sense of fragility, the staff works against it, vigorously encouraging and celebrating any expression of individuality: Helen's complaining, Doona's dancing, my mother's refusal to go to the beauty parlor. They don't deny that it is sad that people end up this way, but rather than pity the person, they respect the effort it takes to be old, not just enduring the obvious losses of youth or a regard for the cumulative struggle of all those years, but they understand how very difficult it is to concentrate on walking, or talking, and sometimes just on breathing . . . lasting.

So now I dance with all the old people. My mother's decline has changed me. I behave differently even with

Sadie and Max, my husband's oldest relatives, who had lived in my neighborhood. I've known them for a good part of my life -- since I was nine years old -- and never liked them.

They had ways of underscoring what was missing in our lives. Standing in front of our building, like sentinels assigned to our stoop, they'd watch and comment when my mother and I were together, making not too subtle innuendoes about my father's not escorting her -- he'd be in the kitchen playing chess. About my trip to Europe, Sadie spread the word that I'd gone to have an abortion. "She is declass," I would tell my husband and others, "a joke."

Suddenly I find I am sympathetic toward them, upset when I see others use that knowing sneer I used to make when the old folks repeated a self-aggrandizing story. Suddenly, I want to buy them a VCR to relieve their boredom. I agree when my husband drives an hour out of the way to take them home. "Of course, we'll take them," I say. I have changed. It is not that I am more considerate; my basic response to old people has changed.

I, the inveterate New Yorker, who interrupts constantly to show I am with a speaker, alongside him, find myself patiently listening to old people, waiting for them to organize their thoughts. I am amazed that I can no longer be angry with them. "Because they are in their late 80's, because they are old . . . for that reason alone . . . they deserve a medal?" someone asks me.

"Yes," I say, and I am surprised that I believe it.

At family gatherings now, when I see how alert they are; when I hear them give detailed directions, when I hear them banter, the pleasure I feel shocks me. I feel the way I do when I see grouse in the woods. I feel the ephemerality of our lives.

A Different Mother

XIX

The Staff Cheers

I go on with my routine, although my mother is always on my mind, even as I speak to Sadie or Max, or shop at the supermarket. On a cold clear December morning, just as I arrive at the school where I am taking a course, the secretary has sought me out. "Rena," she says, "there's a call for you." I wonder who it can be. It is Morningside House.

This is highly unusual. Did I give them the number? I don't remember. This must be it, I think as I rush to the phone.

"Don't worry," the voice says. No, I think, I'm not worried; I know what must happen. "Your mother is okay," the voice continues.

"She is in no pain, but her condition has changed. She will be seen by the doctor at about two in the afternoon."

I am cool, calm, and collected. Her health for the past four months has been declining rapidly, with occasional spurts of energy. She had made the decision "to be helped a little . . . and what will be, will be." Now she will be kept comfortable and not sent to the hospital anymore. Actually, I have been waiting for this call. Yet I am surprised at the dryness in my mouth, the weakness in my legs, and most of all, my resistance to take on the job of having to bury my mother.

I know that if a person dies you are not told that over the phone. So I decide to go to her immediately. I find my mother sleeping peacefully in a clean fresh bed. I can see her breathing. The bed is so white, I think of how she loves clean sheets, and of a day in the snow -- dinner, a hot bath, cocoa -- topped off by clean sheets. Then to celebrate the sweetness, she would tell the story of Cossacks riding through the night to see their betrothed, to catch the household at night with the bedding exposed, to see if the sheets are clean.

I remember her imitating a Cossack. She may have been ironing, but it seemed she held the horses' reins and added, "He wanted to know what the house looked like at night, to see the house in a splendid disorder," and her eyes shone, hinting at what else the night brought, as she explained her theory -- that the attention paid to the bedding would tell how good his time in bed would be.

I watch my mother breathe, her face flushed from the oxygen, and feel her warm hands, and smooth her soft white hair in a neat, still bed.

A nurse enters the room, greets me quietly, and rubs her forefinger on my mother's hand. She calls to her, "Mrs. Trefman, Mrs. Trefman, your daughter's here," and the nurse looks at me and nods, as if to say, "See, no response."

Then the head nurse comes in and tells me how, just the day before, she had taken my mother to the Hanukah party. She shows me how, when my mother was asked if she wanted to go, she had squared her shoulders, and the nurse squared her own, patting each shoulder with her fingertips, imitating my mother. "And then," the nurse pauses, "she shook her head and said, 'absolutely.' She said, 'absolutely' she would go."

The nurse smiles as she tells me this, proud of my mother's strength and of how she had maintained her character and did not weakly acquiesce, or withdraw. This was probably because Rhoda, the secretary who ran the Hanukah party, was going to sing and had asked that my mother attend.

Rhoda, a heavy woman, usually wears a gold ring on each finger. She has a beautiful voice, and when she sings the prayers, fierce disbelievers like my mother become spiritually transformed.

"Oh, 'absolutely' is her word. Yes, I believe she said that," I say, appreciating the story while I eye my mother, not quite sure if she is alive.

The nurse puts her finger to her lips. "Be careful, she can hear," she whispers. Later on in the afternoon, a nurse's aide comes by to take her blood pressure. The doctor comes by; "Mrs. Trefman, Mrs. Trefman," he calls, holding her hand in his, shaking his head and looking to me when there is no response. When I press him for a time frame -- I will have to alert my family -- he says, "I'm no prophet, but no later than the end of the week."

We stay in the pale blue room. The late afternoon sun prints the shadow of tree branches on the wall, and the green oxygen tank bubbles softly.

Rhoda hears of the change in my mother's condition, and enters her room. By then, four of us are standing near my mother's bed. Rhoda starts to weep. I ask her to sing, as much for the comfort of her voice as to stop her crying, which I do not understand. I am ready and dry-eyed. Rhoda sings a prayer. We lose our stoic pose and lean against the wall, relax, and enjoy the luxury of this parting. The tension, our tight grip on mortality, loosens, and like a mist floats out of the room. Rhoda sings another song, *"Ya aseh sholom"* ("Go In Peace").

Suddenly my mother stirs; the doctor jerks to attention. Rhoda keeps on singing; my mother becomes agitated. The four of us lean forward, intently absorbed as we watch her reach for Rhoda's hand, grasp it tightly, and then open her eyes.

"Anna, how are you?" the nurse asks.

"Very well," she answers.

"I cannot sing," the doctor says.

"Mommale, so good to see you," I say, my eyes no longer dry.

"Yes, it's good," she answers weakly, but clearly.

My mother continues to do well that day and the next day also. The staff greets me with cheers, "Well, what do you say about your Momma? She's wonderful."

A Different Mother

XX

I Believe Her Story

Visiting my mother at Morningside House, I almost
think she will fool the angel of death once more. However,
I come every day after that. On the days I come alone she
is alert enough to ask for Laura and Ralph. She seems
sharp and clear. Karen Taylor, her nurse, says, "I love it
when she proves those doctors wrong." I am told that
Rhoda has been coming up to sing to her twice each day.
At Morningside House they cheer her efforts for life.

A sense of urgency and inevitability stirs up
questions I have left alone. I will have to compose my own
answers. Two years have gone by since my mother has
really begun to fail. In those same two years, the visit with
Shoshana started me thinking about an affair between her
father and my mother. The facts are still mixed up,
especially my place in it. Will I ever be able to sort them
out? I wonder, am I Baruch's child, Shoshana's half sister?

On Thursday of the third week in December, as I leave her room she calls out my name in a firm voice. Immediately I go back to her, greeting her again as I enter; she is sitting upright and turns toward me, smiling. I think, it was a happy memory, and this is my last chance to know. I decide I will ask her.

"Mom?"

"Yes, my dear." With the bed raised, she looks as if she is presiding over her realm; she seems comfortable and strong. I MUST ASK HER . . . .

"Tell me, did Poppa know about you and Baruch?" There, I had asked her, as bluntly as I had the first time.

Suddenly her expression changes. She looks around turning her head to the right and to the left, her eyes seeking. "Did you tell Poppa? Did you tell him?" she asks me. My father has been dead for over thirty years.

"No, Mom, I want to know." She lifts her head from the pillow.

"Baruch and I -- we did the right thing. We kept our families whole. We did it *all* the right way. We did it right," and she leans back purposefully. She does not fall back. She does not say anything more.

That was as much as I'd ever know from her.

I remember once a friend's husband had walked out on her and their young baby. The friend was devastated. My mother, to console her, said, "Don't feel all bad. Look at your beautiful baby. He's proof there was something real -- that it was right."

"No baby is an accident," she had said that other time. "Every baby is wanted, even when you wouldn't dare -- something in you wants that baby." I knew that she'd had more than one abortion. But she'd told me many times that she had chosen not to abort me -- and how smart she'd been -- because I was so good. She smiled whenever she told me that story. Now she said their love had been right as well. They had done the right thing. Yes.

"We did it right," she had said to me. Both men were dead; I was alive. It was no accident. This was the legacy I had sought.

*   *   *

That is as close to the facts as I will ever get, and they continue to haunt me. Although Shoshana writes many letters, I cannot send my question through the mail. While my mother lives, Shoshana's letters, between pages of information about her family and questions about mine, urge me to ask my mother about her brother, Aaron. But I do not; I don't want to add to the well of pain his name evokes, even if it may supply another clue.

Today, having heard my mother's declaration, "We did the right thing," I want Shoshana to tell me what she knows, and I promise myself that I will ask her when I see her again. I hope she will make it easy for me.

On Friday Zach arrives from London and visits with Alex, his Russian friend. My mother greets him, "Hello, Zach." They see that she is tired and sit and read Pushkin to her. They talk a little. Three hours later, my son kisses my mother and says, "Good-bye Nannawanni."

"I'll be back," she answers.

As full as my mother's life has been, as ready as I am for her death, I expect more time. David comes down from Boston to see her. He talks to her about her blintzes, her pies, and how she'd cut up oranges for the children to eat.

I have called my sister twice, once to say death was imminent, and then that my mother is better. She does not want to be too late . . . there have been so many false alarms . . . and she has deadlines to meet. She wants to come, but if there is time . . . .

On Saturday, when I get there, Tony, an aide, compliments her tight grasp. "See how strong she is," he says.

"Tony loves you," I say to her.

"And I love them all," she says.

On Sunday, the nurse tells us, "This morning your mother said she is in New York, not in America as she usually says." They had raised her bed. It looks as if she is sitting. The day is cloudy and, even with the lamp on the room, looks dreary. To cheer her up, I tell my mother that I spoke to my sister on the phone, and that she is doing well and coming in from California to see her. She smiles, repeats, "She's coming," and lets out a garbled wail. Laura nods, "Yes, Nannawanni, Bernice is coming."

She looks at my daughter, "I love you, my dear," she

says. Then she grasps my hand and kisses it twice, hard.
We leave. Laura says, "She is not doing better."

That night, having eaten her dinner, my mother
jokes with the aide and goes to sleep. At nine-thirty, on a
bed check, the aide hears my ninety-year-old mother
release her last breath.

The nursing home invites us to have our funeral
services there. "So many admired her," Earl, her social
worker, says. "They will want to come."

I will always be amazed that she was able to evoke
that response from total strangers in her last years, a
phantom of her indomitable person. In so many ways it
had been a bonus year. She had discovered that people
could be trusted. She was able to let her guard down, to
show compassion.

My discoveries are no less remarkable: her romance
. . . my place in it. The slightest reminder evokes deep
sighs.

I've come to see my mother in a bright light. I had
always believed she was so open and impulsive, but clearly
she was discreet and restrained. And yes, absolutely, loyal.

The summer after her death an opportunity presents
itself to find out more about my mother's love affair.
Shoshana and I are walking along Madison Avenue in New
York. Shoshana tells me a curious story. Along that
splendor of stores and summer sun, shadows sharp on the
sidewalks, she describes the mourning period for my

211

mother's baby brother Aaron, the *sheva*, before I was born, almost 60 years earlier. Shoshana was only a little girl; the grown-ups, talking among themselves, unaware that Shoshana was listening, allude to a love affair my grandmother had on the boat on her way to America. They said that Aaron was the child of that affair. "His death," one grown-up had said, "was God's punishment."

I realize that Shoshana wants me to hear that not all babies were conceived in a matrimonial bed. My mother had told me that Aaron was born in Europe, though it wasn't a secret that one aunt had to run away to America where she delivered a healthy, large, though "early" baby. Or that the other, pursuing her lover, delivered a son on the steps of the American embassy in Palestine. Such things happened in our family.

But clearly, Aaron's is the only story Shoshana insists on telling -- not the one I am so eager to hear. Her voice is authoritative, its tone is light, but so conclusive I dare not challenge her. I have lost my nerve and am suddenly on guard, afraid that harsh justice, like Aaron's, will be meted out in my case as well. I do not ask.

I barely remember my grandmother, but as Shoshana speaks, I realize that the two faces could have been images in a mirror: my mother's in that white bed at Morningside House and my grandmother's, in my early memory where she always seemed old and withered, although she was only 72 years old when she died.

Shoshana remembers her differently, calling her,

"my adopted grandmother." "Your grandmother," she goes
on, "was really amazing, livelier than your mother, but
something went out of her after Aaron died." This sounds
right.

On a visit to my aunt's house, I'd read a tall book of
Aesops's Fables with my grandmother, to help her learn
English. Shoshana asks me to imagine a love affair for
that old woman, but that is not the love affair that I am
concerned with.

Later, in the fall, I am at my cousin Ann's house and
see the very same tall Aesop's Fable book, which prompts
me to ask her about Shoshana's story. Seated, at the
dining room table with our husbands and children, Ann
agrees that Aaron had been born in Russia. As for Baruch
and my mother, she responds quickly, "They were friends;
the two families were friends, very good friends, that was
all." I was surprised that she said this. A year earlier she
had agreed that they could have been lovers.

The Talmud forbids one to speak badly of the dead,
so it's possible Ann doesn't want to accuse my mother or
grandmother of an infidelity in front of others. When I tell
her my suspicion about my genesis she chastises me, "What
credence are you giving to the fantasies of an old senile
woman?"

But I also believe that that is where the truth is:
that senility removes the societal scrim, like a window
shade that conceals a visiting lover and suddenly rolls up
to reveal his embrace. When my mother spoke to me

during those two years, and then again at the very end, I believed what she said.

At the funeral service, Rhoda sings. The rabbi, who knew my mother at Morningside, meets with Bernice and me to talk about my mother, before the service. His eulogy respects our sense of her, gently recounting a visit with Bernice. I listen as he applauds my mother's strength at Morningside House. The rabbi tenderly persuades us that, except for Simon's death, she would not have liked her life remembered as a hard life: for her, it was victorious.

XXI

Nannawanni Pie

The next day, for the first time, Laura, Carol, Bernice, and I, together, make her famous apple pie -- the heavy crust is sweet cookie dough, the filling tart.

It comes out perfect.

A Different Mother

Acknowledgements

Early on, stories, poems, muddled events -- and family mysteries -- hidden in childhood notebooks were a private source of comfort. Writing clarified what and how I thought, opening myself to myself. Soon small bits and stories were published. Short stories would become chapters in the memoir -- a project nurtured by many parents.

The book was born when Alan Gelb, an author and playwright, led a seminar class at Montclair State College in the 1980s. The assignment was to write a one-page biography. I wrote a story about my mother. He called me to his desk and said, "There is a book here."

Now, about thirty years later, my daughter-in-law Carol Lin, who knew that despite a few encouraging rejections my book lay locked away in a box, unpublished, said, "Do it now," and quickly added, "I'll help you publish." She is a woman who gets things done. The proof is that you, the reader, are here!

The book, or more accurately the journey, began the

day my son, Zach, met a former schoolmate on the train commuting to NYC. She directed me to my first writing group in Montclair, New Jersey, and to Gail Kaliss, a kind, brilliant and generous woman. In time, Gail and I literally built a unique relationship, as I helped her renovate her house while she guided me with literary and grammatical tools. Jim Nash's course at Montclair State followed. A strong advocate of the 'free-write,' he admonished us, "Never lift the pencil off the page," and so I found my real-self on paper. He directed me to Susanna Rich's writing group. She included an essay of mine, published in the *New York Times*, in her textbook *The Flexible Writer*. Although I had no plan, I kept writing, enjoying my new-found writing skills.

I knew I had a lot to learn. I enrolled at Rutgers for literature courses and caught up with works I'd missed, hungry to grasp author references in the *New York Times Book Review*. In Ann Sobel's class, along with studying Edith Wharton's *Age of Innocence* and Virginia Woolf's *Mrs. Dalloway*, we developed a warm friendship. With Ann, I found the courage not to edit concerns that surfaced as I wrote, concerns which became major threads in this memoir.

I had heard about a new program at Sarah Lawrence for women going back to school, where I worked with Joan Peters and finally followed through on Alan Gelb's heartfelt advice.

These are the parents of the book, and I am most grateful to them.

Then the book rested. My mother was failing. I was the only child close enough to be there for her. I wobbled between new-found strengths and pained witness of my mother's condition. Gradually, little steps, lucky accidents, desire, and fear melded. Afraid I'd lose the powerful stew that made up a childhood crammed with songs, proverbs, Yiddish and 'struggles-overcome,' I began to work in earnest. Years later, after my mother died, the late poet Enid Dame encouraged romantic elements -- asked key questions and gave sweet applause. I worked hard. The writing was done.

However, without the urging and nudging, the both critical and loving reactions of friends, my mother's fans, I doubt that I would have kept on. Annette Ostro kept at me: "That lady needs a book." Sandy Levine, with whom I shared our first cigarette; Elaine Abrams who says she can still smell my mother's apple pie; Emily Nelson, a writing group member, whose writing comments and "perfect potato salad" recipe are lingering gifts -- all sustained me. The poet Bracha Nechama Bomze, a young cousin who recently published *Love Justice*, and Pia Licciardi Abate, co-author of a new Frank Lloyd Wright book, both inspired me; and, miraculously, Ann Eisenstodt, a dear friend, both poet and artist, offered to design the book and insisted I "get it done!" Gail Kaliss, now in Anchorage, Alaska, her generous nature still intact, kindly and carefully edited and formatted this final version.

Many thanks to Morningside for the caring attention they gave my mother, and for the compassion that filled the halls for both residents and family. I was amazed and grateful to learn how full of richness and resilience the end of life can be.

Oh, friends, neighbors who cared, to list you all would out-print the book. You know who you are, and that I love you still.

I thank my wonderful children, Laura, Zach, and David, for their place in the story and most delightfully in my life; and Carol, who sparked the book out of a box to a published book; and my six grandchildren, Dora, Tess,

Adam, Yasmina, Layla, and Jamila, whom my mother would have enjoyed. And my darling husband, Ralph, whose gifts shifted from nightgowns and pocketbooks to a silver pen and leather notebook.

Made in the USA
Columbia, SC
12 January 2018